SURVIVING FRESHMAN YEAR

GREGORY JONES

Copyright 2022

MSI Press LLC
1760 Airline Hwy, #203
Hollister, CA 95023

All rights reserved. No part of this book may be reproduced or utilized in any form or by any means, digital or mechanical, including photocopying, recording, or by any information and retrieval system, without permission in writing from the publisher.

Copyeditor: Lynne Curry

Book design: Opeyemi Ikuborije

Cover photo: Shutterstock: emerald_media

ISBN: 9781957354163

Library of Congress Control Number: 2022915734

CONTENTS

CHAPTER 1: *Freshman Orientation* 1

CHAPTER 2: *Sunday Lunch* 11

CHAPTER 3: *Student Workers* 25

CHAPTER 4: *Thanksgiving Break* 37

CHAPTER 5: *Christmas Break* 49

CHAPTER 6: *When You Don't Quite Fit In* 63

CHAPTER 7: *Spring Break* 73

CHAPTER 8: *Goodbye Winter, Hello Spring!* 83

CHAPTER 9: *Leadership Team* 95

CHAPTER 10: *The Catalyst* 105

CHAPTER 11: *Dead Week Decisions* 115

CHAPTER 12: *Going Home, Leaving Home* 125

Notes for Discussion Leaders 137

CHAPTER 1

Freshman Orientation

Brandon watched as his family drove away and then turned toward his residence hall. He thought about the road that lay in front of him. He was about to begin life as a college freshman. Brandon thought about all the new people he was about to meet. There would be new classes, campus organizations, and events to attend. There would also be freedom. He would be responsible for many of his own choices now. This was exciting, but it also made Brandon nervous.

As Brandon walked up the front stairwell to his new home, Cordell Hall, he thought about his life up to this point. He grew up in a small town with a high school that had just over 600 students. His new university had over 20,000. The families in his hometown had lived there for generations. This new campus would have a diverse group of students from across the country. In high school, his classes centered around the basic subjects of math, science, history, and language arts, with some opportunities for sports and the creative arts. Now he would have a seemingly endless list of majors from which to choose.

His support system would also be different. Brandon had known his friends since his first year of school. Very few of them would be attending here. Now he would be meeting new people in his residence hall, in his classes, and any organizations he chose to join. His family had raised him in a church where there were other kids his age. He had received solid teaching and formed strong friendships there. Now he would be looking for a new church home to serve as a source of support.

Brandon entered his room to find his roommate, Austin, still unpacking his clothes. Austin seemed like a good guy. Brandon and Austin, along with their parents, had gotten to know each other while helping the boys move in and eating lunch together. Brandon found out that Austin also grew up in a smaller town and they had more in common than he first thought. Neither of them owned a car, but the school had a bookstore, post office, and cafeteria. The school also had a transit service that ran to a shopping center, grocery store, and a few other locations near campus.

"How did it go with the goodbyes?" Austin asked.

"It was alright until my mom started crying," Brandon answered.

"My mom did, too. I didn't know what to do," Austin said.

Brandon nodded. "Nothing you can do. Just wait it out."

Austin looked around the room. "It's going to take some work to make this look as good as it does in the brochure."

"I know, right?" Brandon laughed. "In the advertisements for campus, they make these rooms look like luxury suites.

But I saw a flyer in the lobby for a neighborhood yard sale next weekend. Maybe we could find some stuff to decorate the room."

"That would give us a week to settle in. By then, we would know where the bare spots are."

"Plus, maybe we could see how some of the other rooms are set up, especially the rooms with guys who lived here last year."

Austin had finished getting his shirts and pants put away and was now working on his underclothes. "I've never really had to think about how to set up my own space. My family has always lived in the same house so my room has always been about the same."

"Same here," Brandon said. "We moved once when I was a baby, but I don't even remember the house where we lived before. Really, this is about the biggest move I've ever made."

"What's the longest you've ever been away from home?" Austin asked.

Brandon thought for a moment. "I usually went to a camp during the summer. And some family vacations. But really never more than a week or two at a time. How about you?"

"About the same. One summer we visited some family in Texas. My dad wanted to drive and see some other sights along the way. It ended up being a two-week trip."

"Whew!" Brandon exclaimed. "That's a lot of togetherness in the car."

"Yeah," Austin said. "You really learn how important deodorant is when you spend the majority of your day stuck in a car driving across the country."

They both laughed and continued unpacking.

SURVIVING FRESHMAN YEAR

They were still working on their room when they heard a knock at the door. Chris and Matt lived in the room next door. They had come by to ask if Brandon and Austin wanted to walk down to the student center with them. It was almost time for the start of Coming Attractions.

Coming Attractions was the university's orientation program for new students. The theme was based on the previews that are shown before a movie. Student leaders were dressed in uniforms similar to what employees wore at movie theaters, making it easy to find a student leader if you needed help. Representatives of campus organizations would be available to talk one on one with students about their specific organizations.

Brandon talked with many of the group representatives. There were academic-based organizations, representatives of the different sports offered by the university, various campus ministries, sororities and fraternities, and service clubs. Each of these clubs would be having events over the first few weeks of school where students could attend and see which of them were the best fit.

After speaking with many of the groups represented, Brandon found three groups that he wanted to try. These were the University Resident's Council, Be the Change, and Campus Christian Assembly. The Resident's Council was a group focused on addressing the needs of students living on campus. Be the Change was a group based on volunteering and service opportunities both on and off campus. Campus Christian Assembly was a campus ministry that served as a place for students of faith to gather, fellowship, and engage in service activities. Brandon decided he would visit each of the

4

group's introductory meetings being held over the next two weeks.

The student leaders of Coming Attractions divided students into small groups for campus tours. Brandon, Austin, Chris, and Matt all were part of the same group. The tour proved to be very helpful in finding where their classes were as well as the most efficient routes to get from one class to the next. Brandon was relieved to see Lauren, a friend from high school, included in the tour group. Lauren had the advantage of already living on campus for a week. The university had an excellent music program, and Lauren was part of the marching band. Students belonging to the band had moved into campus a week before everyone else to begin practicing for the halftime shows at upcoming football games. Lauren offered to show Brandon some of the other areas of campus that were not heavily focused on during the Coming Attractions tours.

As the tour concluded, everyone headed back to the student center. The rest of the day was going to be busy. Student groups would rotate between being issued their student ID's, having some time to visit the bookstore, and updating some information to their online university accounts. Brandon was naturally anxious about deciding which group or groups to join. He was concerned with whether or not he would be able to make new friends. Would anyone like him? Would he be able to fit in? His thoughts immediately turned to his friends from high school, and although he had not been at his new school a full day, he already missed home. There were some big decisions ahead of Brandon. He just hoped he made the right ones.

Scripture

Proverbs 3:5–6

Trust in the LORD with all your heart
and lean not on your own understanding;
in all your ways submit to him,
and he will make your paths straight.

Hebrews 13:8

Jesus Christ is the same yesterday and today and forever.

Matthew 6:25-34

Therefore, I tell you, do not worry about your life, what you will eat or drink; or about your body, what you will wear. Is not life more than food, and the body more than clothes? Look at the birds of the air; they do not sow or reap or store away in barns, and yet your heavenly Father feeds them. Are you not much more valuable than they? Can any one of you by worrying add a single hour to your life?

And why do you worry about clothes? See how the flowers of the field grow. They do not labor or spin. Yet I tell you that not even Solomon in all his splendor was dressed like one of these. If that is how God clothes the grass of the field, which is here today and tomorrow is thrown into the fire, will he not much more clothe you—you of little faith? So do not worry, saying, 'What shall we eat?' or 'What shall we drink?' or 'What shall we wear?' For the pagans run after all these things, and your heavenly Father knows that you need them. But seek first his kingdom and his righteousness, and all these things will be given to you as well. Therefore, do not worry about tomorrow, for tomorrow will worry about itself. Each day has enough trouble of its own.

John 14:15-17

If you love me, keep my commands. And I will ask the Father, and he will give you another advocate to help you and be with you forever—the Spirit of truth. The world cannot accept him, because it neither sees him nor knows him. But you know him, for he lives with you and will be in you.

SURVIVING FRESHMAN YEAR

Questions

1. When was a time in your life you felt uncertain about how a situation would turn out? What happened as you went through it?

2. Who can you reach out to when you face difficulty in life? Sometimes in these times, it can be difficult to trust God. How do you respond to times when it is difficult to trust God?

3. In the story, Brandon faced a lot of uncertainty. Which of his concerns do you identify most with? Why?

4. What are some concerns you have about beginning college that were not mentioned in Brandon's story? Each year of college brings unique challenges. If you are not a freshman, what are some of the concerns you had about starting this school year?

5. Change is a constant throughout life. Consider the following as you review the scripture for this chapter:

   a. Proverbs 3:5-6. With some of the challenges you face this school year, what would it look like to trust in the Lord as you deal with these difficulties them?

   b. Hebrews 13:8. Do you find it easy to believe this verse about the unchanging nature of Jesus? How can this verse reassure us as we deal with lives full of so much change?

c. Matthew 6:2-34. What can you learn about God's provision from these verses? In life, we are going to have legitimate concerns, such as choosing a career and budgeting our time and resources. According to this passage, how can we handle concerns about the future without worrying?

d. John 14:15-17. Jesus has asked God to provide the Holy Spirit as a helper. As you face various troubles, how can this verse reassure you that you are not alone?

6. Brandon faces a choice concerning which student groups to join. Which factors would be most important in deciding which group or groups to join? What would you do if you were in Brandon's place?

Challenge for the Week

Think of one specific thing you can do this semester to meet new people. It might be seeking out a campus organization to join or as simple as getting to know some people in your classes, your residence halls, or your apartment complex.

CHAPTER 2

Sunday Lunch

Austin barely got to work on time. He had been out late the night before with Brandon and some others they met through a college-age Bible study sponsored by a local church they attended. Austin usually went to church with his family on Christmas and Easter but had never been a regular attender. Brandon had invited him, and it seemed like a good way to make new friends. Austin was enjoying the study and had made new friends, and they had enjoyed a fantastic game of capture the flag the night before. They had gathered at the church playground, which bordered an open field and a wilderness trail. The students had divided into two groups with each group choosing a base on opposite sides of the church. The object of the game was simple: The first group to get the other team's flag and return it to the spot where their flag was located would be the winner. What made this really fun was the inclusion of water guns. Everyone had a water gun to spray members of the opposite team. If you got hit, you had

11

SURVIVING FRESHMAN YEAR

to return to your team's flag and start over.

The game went much more slowly than Austin expected since everyone tried to stay out of sight while approaching the other team's flag. It was already dark, and everyone moved slowly while trying not to make any noise. Although Austin's team lost one more game than they won, everyone on both teams had a great time.

Austin rubbed his eyes and clocked in. He worked at a local restaurant and Sunday lunch was one of the busiest times of the week. It was 10 a.m., and he started getting his section ready for the lunch rush. Since he started attending church, Austin would normally be there, but a condition of this job was weekend availability. Although he had worked at the restaurant for a couple of weeks, this would be his first Sunday lunch shift.

Something the other employees were saying to Austin confused him. While getting to know his coworkers, Austin had mentioned that he had started attending church. Now his coworkers kept referring to the customers that would be coming for Sunday lunch as "your people." It was clear this was not meant as a compliment. Austin could not figure out why everyone was dreading this lunch shift so much. When the doors were unlocked at 11a.m. and customers began arriving, everything became clear.

Austin was hosting for the first hour of his shift and would then start serving customers. The first to arrive was a family of four, two adults and two teenage children. A man and teenage boy both had on khaki pants and polo shirts. The mother and teenage girl both had on dresses. Austin guessed from this that they had just come from church. They approached the host's stand where Austin greeted them and

12

began walking them back. The mother saw the row of booths they were approaching and loudly objected.

"I do *not* want any of these booths! They are too close to the kitchen. The last time we were here, I couldn't hear myself think for all the noise coming out of there."

Austin was calm and professional. "I'd be glad to find you another place to sit. Right this way."

He escorted the family to a booth further from the kitchen. "Will this work for you?" he asked.

The woman said, "This is much better."

The family sat down. Austin handed them menus. "Your server will be right with you."

Austin paused for a moment and left when he realized no one was going to say anything else. The family didn't have to thank him for finding them another seat, but he had expected them to as a general courtesy. He had also paused rather than walking away because most customers would say thank you or at least smile and nod that they had heard him. Simply turning and leaving seemed rude to him. However, when everyone just looked down at their menus, he suddenly felt very awkward and just left.

The next family he greeted was shifting back and forth impatiently when he greeted them. There were two men and a female in this group, also dressed in clothing that told Austin they were coming from church."

"Good morning. How many will be in your party today?"

"Where have you been? We've been waiting for five minutes!" exclaimed one of the men.

"I'm sorry. I needed to find my last party a different seat," Austin explained. He thought about the time spent with the previous family. Even with finding them an acceptable booth,

SURVIVING FRESHMAN YEAR

he couldn't have been away from the host stand more than three minutes. In reality, it probably wasn't even two minutes. But he held his tongue. "After all," he thought sarcastically to himself, "the customer is always right." Thankfully, this party did not object to the booth where Austin seated them.

Every group that came in had clearly come from church. Austin figured these families must have gone to the early service. He chuckled as he thought that they might be in a better mood if they had slept in and gone to the late service.

A group of three elderly ladies came in next. As they slowly came in through the lobby, Austin glanced out at the dining area. Each server had a cluster of tables in order to keep watch over his or her customers. Each party that Austin seated went to a different server, so no one became overwhelmed. Austin looked at the next section to be seated for an open table.

Austin greeted the ladies and began leading them back.

"We can't go that far!" one of the ladies exclaimed.

"We always sit at one of these tables," another said, pointing at a group of tables close to the lobby.

"Of course. How will this table be?" Austin asked the ladies.

They sat and were given their menus. Austin excused himself and returned to the host stand. He had an odd feeling he was being watched, and he quickly realized why. Roger, one of the servers, was staring him down as he approached Austin.

"You just gave me another table! Janie was next to be seated," Roger informed him.

"They wanted a table up front," Austin said, defending himself.

"Fine, whatever," Roger said as he let out an audible sigh and stormed off.

14

Austin understood why Roger was aggravated. It was tough on a server to get two tables at once, but he had not done it on purpose. He stayed calm. His coworkers knew he went to church so he was determined to model a good attitude. The attitude of the customers, however, had totally caught him off guard.

At noon, Travis and Melissa came in to take over hosting. As the full lunch crowd would be arriving, more servers came in, and the full dining area began being seated. Austin was ready to begin serving.

The customers seated in his section were some of the rudest people Austin had ever seen! Just as with the customers he sat while hosting, it was clear to Austin that the families now being sat in his section had just come from church. Austin made an effort to greet each table quickly and take their drink order. Despite this prompt greeting, many customers shifted in their seats and sighed as if they had been waiting an eternity. Some ordered their drinks without looking at Austin or acknowledging him as a person. One family asked if they got a discount with a church bulletin. Austin apologized and said they didn't before excusing himself to get their drinks.

This went on for the next hour. The church crowd seemed terribly grumpy to Austin. Soon his section was full. He got each table's order in and food out to those whose orders were ready. He took a moment to go back to the host's station. He saw people sitting in the lobby and knew there was now a wait to be seated. A customer was waving her arms at Travis and Melissa, who both looked defeated.

"You know it's going to be busy on Sunday. Why aren't you prepared for this?"

"I'm sorry for your wait," Melissa said.

Travis said, "It should only be about 15 minutes, and we'll have a place for you."

Austin thought better than to get involved and just kept walking. It was amazing how upset some customers became after being told there would be a 15-minute wait.

One large group was given a longer wait due to the table size they would need, and an elderly woman in the group was letting the host know very loudly how upset she was about the longer wait. She would instantly point out when any smaller party that arrived after them was called to be seated.

As the food was ready to go to Austin's customers, he asked if there was anything else they needed. This question led to a nightmare situation for Austin. Customers seemed like they could only ask for one thing at a time. At one table, a man asked for extra ketchup. When Austin brought it, a woman at the same table asked for extra napkins. Austin brought the napkins, and a third person at the table asked for steak sauce. Austin was happy to help. This was his job, but running back and forth for one item at a time kept him from his other tables. From the way his other tables were behaving when Austin checked on them, he knew that his absence would not be treated with any degree of understanding.

Despite these challenges, Austin made an effort to provide each guest with great service. He had treated each person with respect, smiling even when met with rudeness by some and indifference by others. Some were polite and interacted with Austin in a more pleasant way. But these were the minority. At first, he was sure the grouchy families were just grumpy because they were hungry. As the day went on, though, he realized that only a few of his tables gave him any kind of recognition.

It was at least encouraging to think about the large bills that these families would get, which would hopefully lead to generous tips. Unfortunately, that source of hope was quickly extinguished. As the first few tables finished their meals and left, Austin was shocked to find that many tables had only left a few dollars as a tip. The bill and credit card receipts both had 10%, 15%, and 20% tips calculated for customers. Despite the math being done for them and receiving excellent service, the collective Sunday lunch crown proved to be horribly low tippers. Austin could not believe what he had just experienced.

Then, something even stranger happened. A second wave of customers came in around 2 p.m. Austin's coworkers explained that this was the non-churchgoing crowd. They had probably slept in and were getting a late start to their day. They were more casually dressed, and their attitude was also more relaxed. As Austin greeted his tables, he found them to be much more pleasant than the church crowd.

Austin greeted his first table. They were talking and laughing but stopped and looked at Austin. "How are you today?" one of them asked. Austin was startled. This was the first customer all day to greet him in such a positive way.

As they left, they were also good natured. One man said, "Hope you get out of here in time to enjoy this beautiful day." Austin also found the midafternoon customers to be better tippers.

When his shift was over, Austin began thinking through what he had just experienced. He had been raised to treat people with respect. The customers were there to be served, but that shouldn't entitle them to treat the employees so terribly. And his coworkers were calling this group "his people." He caught the transit back to campus, and during

SURVIVING FRESHMAN YEAR

the ride Austin thought of a recent discussion in his Bible study group. The discussion revolved around being part of the church. The physical building was just the meeting place of the church. It was up to each person to take the church into his or her community. Austin asked himself how he could make a positive influence for Christ when the group his coworkers dreaded the most were Christians. He also struggled to make sense of how the nonchurchgoers were so much more pleasant.

Scripture

Philippians 1:27-28

Whatever happens, conduct yourselves in a manner worthy of the gospel of Christ. Then, whether I come and see you or only hear about you in my absence, I will know that you stand firm in the one Spirit, striving together as one for the faith of the gospel without being frightened in any way by those who oppose you. This is a sign to them that they will be destroyed, but that you will be saved—and that by God.

2 Corinthians 1:12

Now this is our boast: Our conscience testifies that we have conducted ourselves in the world, and especially in our relations with you, with integrity and godly sincerity. We have done so, relying not on worldly wisdom but on God's grace.

Colossians 3:23-24

Whatever you do, work at it with all your heart, as working for the Lord, not for human masters, since you know that you will receive an inheritance from the Lord as a reward. It is the Lord Christ you are serving.

1 Peter 2:13-17

Submit yourselves for the Lord's sake to every human authority: whether to the emperor, as the supreme authority, or to governors, who are sent by him to punish those who do wrong and to commend those who do right. For it is God's will that by doing good you should silence the ignorant talk of foolish people. Live as free people, but do not use your freedom as a cover-up for evil; live as God's slaves. Show proper respect to everyone, love the family of believers, fear God, honor the emperor.

Questions

1. If you were Austin, tell how would you conduct yourself with each of the following groups:

   - coworkers

   - customers that you may only see once

   - regular customers that you see each week

2. Consider the following as you read the scripture verses for this chapter:

   a. Philippians 1:27-28. Why do you think the way Christians conduct themselves matters? How might you face opposition for conducting yourself in a way that honors God?

   b. 2 Corinthians 1:12. What benefits come from behaving in a way that honors God?

   c. Colossians 3:23-24. Austin's customers may not always appreciate the effort he puts into providing excellent service. What reasons can be found in these verses for Austin to continue striving to provide great service?

   d. 1 Peter 2:13-17. How does submitting to human authority honor God? When would be a time it is not appropriate to submit to an authority figure? Who in your life is it hardest to show respect for?

SURVIVING FRESHMAN YEAR

3. We are not guaranteed to be treated fairly by people with authority over us. This could include family members, teachers, and both supervisors and customers at our jobs. How does the scripture verses from 1 Peter say Christians should conduct themselves?

4. In this chapter, Austin is dealing with difficult customers. Put yourself in their position. The customer should have the benefit of good service. In this chapter, specific behaviors we see include requests for different seating, continuously asking for extra items such as napkins and steak sauce, rude behavior, and poor tipping. Are all of these behaviors necessarily bad? Which ones bother you the most? Why do you think that is?

5. In this chapter, we see examples of rude behavior. Although this behavior is hurtful, no serious damage is done. Unfortunately, sometimes we can be treated in ways that are abusive. There is a difference between simply being treated unfairly and being abused. How would you determine where that line is with the different groups in your life (family, friends, teachers, supervisors, or customers)? What are appropriate actions to take if you feel being treated poorly has crossed that line?

6. Throughout life, you may meet people who have been turned off by Christians because of how they conduct themselves. They may feel that Christians are rude, judgmental, or think they are better than other people. How could you be an effective witness

to those who have this opinion of Christians? What could Austin do to be a positive example for his coworkers?

7. The customers in this chapter do not consider how their actions and attitudes are being viewed by the restaurant staff. Where are some places in your life that others may be observing your behavior?

8. The chapter opened with a story about Austin and his friends playing capture the flag with water guns. Some people may have a misconception that Christians never do anything fun. What could you invite friends to do that would show that being a Christian doesn't mean you aren't allowed to have any fun?

Challenge for the Week

Sometimes our actions can be just as powerful of a witness for Christ as our words. What is something you can do this week to honor God in your actions?

CHAPTER 3

Student Workers

Chris and Matt met Amanda and Hannah for lunch in the cafeteria. They were in the same history class and had become friends. As they ate, they discussed their plans for the weekend. It was homecoming week and everyone was looking forward to Saturday night's football game. Chris and Matt were going to spend the day at the campus carnival set up at the university's amphitheater. There would be carnival games and live music leading up to the football game. Amanda and Hannah would be joining them about an hour before the game.

"I wish I had the whole day off but at least I only work the morning shift," Hannah said.

"Same here," Amanda replied. "I'm just glad we were both able to get Saturday night off."

Hannah and Amanda both worked at a local mall. Hannah worked at a restaurant in the food court while Amanda worked in one of the department stores. The mall was close to campus and the stores employed many students from the university.

"Just text us when you are headed for the stadium," Matt said.

"Sure thing," Amanda replied. "Well, my next class starts soon. I need to get going."

"My study group meets in 15 minutes. I'll walk with you," said Matt.

Everyone said their goodbyes as Amanda and Matt got up and left the cafeteria. Hannah let out a little sigh and looked down at her tray. Chris noticed that Hannah appeared distracted.

"Is everything ok?" he asked. "You look like you have something on your mind."

"I do," said Hannah. "You know how Amanda and I were both looking for campus jobs at the beginning of the semester?"

"Yeah," Chris answered. "I remember you both had applied for all kinds of positions around campus."

"Well, I was studying in the library and saw a flyer advertising a position that just opened up."

"That's great! Where is the job?"

Hannah answered, "It's in the campus ID office. I'd be helping students and staff get new and replacement ID's."

"That's just down the hall from here. It sounds perfect. You'd be close to the bookstore, the cafeteria, and all the student service offices. Plus, you'd be right here on campus."

"Yeah, it's exactly the type of thing I'd been looking for."

"So why don't you seem more upbeat about this?" Chris asked. "Isn't this a good thing?"

"It is. It would be great to get an on-campus job. I could work during some of my longer breaks between classes. And I'd save a lot of time that I spend driving to work now and looking for a parking spot when I get back."

"I don't really see the downside here, Hannah."

"It's Amanda. I'm struggling with whether or not I should tell her about the position. There were lots of people looking for student jobs at the beginning of the semester. Now that we are into the semester, I doubt as many people are watching the on-campus job postings."

"You're probably right," Chris agreed. "Most of the people I know that didn't get on-campus jobs found part time jobs in town. I haven't heard any of them mention that they are still watching for open positions. Once they got their off-campus jobs, they just sort of quit looking."

"Same here," Hannah said. "I think people got into the routine of the semester. They got used to their class and work schedules, even if they had to settle for an off-campus job."

"It makes sense. We are naturally creatures of habit. Plus, I know I've made friends at my job, and I don't mind the work too bad. I've gotten used to it. I mean, if I hated it, then of course I'd be looking for something else. But that would be up to me."

Hannah nodded in agreement. "And I think everyone has a responsibility to check for open jobs and get in their own applications. But I also think about the Golden Rule. If someone else found an open position, I would want them to tell me. So shouldn't I tell Amanda?"

"That's a tough one." Chris sat for a moment, thinking. "You would be creating competition for yourself. Then there is also no guarantee either of you would even be selected for the position. Do you think it would hurt Amanda's feelings if you didn't tell her and then got selected for the position?"

"I don't know. I can say that she hasn't been as diligent about watching for new open positions to be posted. And she already has a job. So, it's not like she would be unemployed if I don't tell her."

"How does she like her job?"

"I know she has made some friends there. And it isn't too busy on weekdays. She has mentioned having some downtime during her shifts in the middle of the week."

"What about you? How do you like your job?" Chris asked.

"I don't. The food court is always busy. I don't want to sound lazy, but it would be nice to have some downtime every once in a while."

"I get it. Some guys in my dorm work in the library. They get to do their homework or study if they get all the returned books put back on the shelves."

"Exactly," Hannah said. "There are lots of positives to this. Another one is that I would only have to work weekends during student orientations."

"Do you think you would get bored? Seems like after school gets started, there wouldn't be much demand for new ID cards."

"I bet there is more than you think. A girl that lives down the hall from me has already lost her ID twice and had to get it replaced. Plus, since we swipe our ID's here at the cafeteria, going into so many buildings, and going into football games, anybody with a damaged ID would need to replace it."

"True. I hadn't thought of that."

Hannah continued. "And beyond just students, any time the school hires a new employee, they'll need an ID too."

"You may be busier than I thought. How long do you have to decide if you are going to tell Amanda?"

"The notice said the job would be open to applicants through the end of business on Friday. I'm putting in my application tomorrow, and that gives me until the end of the week to decide what to do. I just keep going over the Golden Rule in my head. I'm thinking myself in circles."

"You said you weren't sure if it would hurt Amanda's feelings if you didn't tell her about the job. Would it hurt your feelings if your roles were reversed?"

"If the other person knew how much I wanted out of the food court and still didn't tell me, it would."

"Then don't you think you should tell her?"

"Our circumstances are different," Hannah said. "She doesn't mind her job. I also think she enjoys getting the employee discount so she can shop there herself. And like we talked about before, part of this is her responsibility to keep looking if she wants a campus job."

"Do you think she would like working in the ID office?"

"I don't know. She is an extrovert, so I know she wouldn't mind working with all the people that come through getting their ID's."

"I think I'd appreciate being told about the job. Then I could decide for myself if I wanted to apply. But that's just me."

"That's fair," Hannah sighed. "I want to do the right thing, but I also really want out of the food court. Why should I create competition for myself?"

"I'm sorry your job stinks. Good luck with the job and your decision. Let me know what you decide."

Scripture

2 Corinthians 8:21

For we are taking pains to do what is right, not only in the eyes of the Lord but also in the eyes of man.

Matthew 22:34-40

Hearing that Jesus had silenced the Sadducees, the Pharisees got together. One of them, an expert in the law, tested him with this question: "Teacher, which is the greatest commandment in the Law?"

Jesus replied: "'Love the Lord your God with all your heart and with all your soul and with all your mind.' This is the first and greatest commandment. And the second is like it: 'Love your neighbor as yourself.' All the Law and the Prophets hang on these two commandments."

John 15:12

My command is this: Love each other as I have loved you.

Galatians 6:1-6

Brothers and sisters, if someone is caught in a sin, you who live by the Spirit should restore that person gently. But watch yourselves, or you also may be tempted. Carry each other's burdens, and in this way you will fulfill the law of Christ. If anyone thinks they are something when they are not, they deceive themselves. Each one should test their own actions. Then they can take pride in themselves alone, without comparing themselves to someone else, for each one should carry their own load. Nevertheless, the one who receives instruction in the word should share all good things with their instructor.

Questions

1. Tell about a time someone treated you with kindness. How did this make you feel?

2. Tell about a time you treated someone the way you would want to be treated if you were in their position. What motivated you to do what you did?

3. Review the scripture readings one at a time. Consider the following about each passage:

    a. 2 Corinthians 8:21. When we do what is right in the eyes or the Lord, it honors God. What do you think the passage means when it says that it also matters to do what is right in the eyes of man? How can our behavior be an example of Christ's love to those who may be observing our words and actions?

    b. Matthew 22:34-40. When we think of loving others as we love ourselves, we often think of things like being kind and respectful to others. Consider how much emphasis we often put on our own comfort or getting our own way. What would it look like to truly love your neighbor as yourself?

    c. John 15:12. Consider how much Jesus loves us. Remember the suffering he endured and His sacrifice on the cross. How does this impact your view of what it would look like to show Christ's love to each other?

d. Galatians 6:1-6. This passage mentions both carrying each other's burdens and carrying our own load. Imagine our responsibilities and burdens as rocks of different sizes. Some may be boulders that we cannot lift by ourselves. What are some examples of boulders that we cannot carry on our own? Some rocks are smaller and could fit into a backpack that we can carry. What are some examples of these responsibilities that we are to carry for ourselves?

4. Hannah has to decide whether to tell Amanda about the open position. What decision would you make if you were in Hannah's place? If you were in Amanda's place, would you be mad if Hannah didn't tell you about the position, or would you feel that you should have been more active in looking for open positions?

5. We know that Amanda has not taken as much initiative as Hannah to continue searching for open jobs. We also know that Amanda does have a job, but it is just not as convenient as an on-campus job would be. How do these details affect your decision? Are there any other factors you would use in making your decision?

Challenge for the Week

Commit to putting yourself in the place of others you interact with this week. Think about the different rocks and boulders they may be carrying. Consider how you would want to be treated if you were in their position. Examples could include neighbors in your residence hall, customers at work, or something as simple as other drivers on the road.

CHAPTER 4

Thanksgiving Break

A university residence hall can be a lonely place on Thanksgiving Day. All classes were canceled the Wednesday before Thanksgiving so students could travel home for the holiday. There were foreign exchange students still on campus, and the International Student Fellowship had events lined up through the weekend for them. Many students whose families lived locally still spent the long weekend at home so they could enjoy time with family and leftovers from Thanksgiving dinner. The campus was going to be a ghost town.

Daniel would be one of the few people still on campus over Thanksgiving. He was one of the resident advisors (RA's) in Cordell Hall, the residence hall where Brandon, Austin, Chris, and Matt lived. A resident advisor had to be on duty each night and throughout each weekend to assist students living in the residence halls. Even though the residence hall would be almost empty over Thanksgiving, an RA still had to be on duty. Since Daniel lived within an hour of campus, he had actually volunteered for Thanksgiving weekend. He would be able to spend Thanksgiving morning and afternoon with his family before going on duty Thursday evening. He would also visit his family on Friday before going on weekend duty. But starting Friday at 3 p.m., he would be virtually alone in the residence hall for the rest of the weekend.

Daniel had prepared for his time as best he could. There were some class projects due at the end of the semester that he needed to complete. He had borrowed a video game system from another RA, and of course he had access to a few streaming services to watch an almost endless list of TV shows and movies. So, he wasn't too worried about keeping himself occupied.

Unfortunately, Mother Nature had other plans for Daniel. On Thursday night, a huge snowstorm ruined his plans to visit his family on Friday before his weekend duty began. The storm also disabled the internet service to the campus. Daniel found himself unable to do research for his class projects. Cell towers were also impacted by the storm, limiting Daniel's ability to stream movies or even call and text his friends. Even the video game system proved useless since all the games he had borrowed required connecting to the internet to play.

Luckily, the electricity never went out. But an empty residence hall can be surprisingly spooky, even if well lit. Although most students were away, Daniel occasionally walked around the residence hall. RA's were required to periodically check the hallways, exits, and make sure any guests were properly signed in and out. Even with no one in the building, Daniel still took his responsibilities seriously. An added bonus was it allowed him to get some exercise.

As Daniel made his last round on Friday night, he could hear every creak and groan from the walls. Moving through the silent stairwells at each end of the building, Daniel heard the wind howling. Walking down the second-floor hallway, he heard something thump. He turned and looked back. He almost spoke out to ask who was there. Was it just the building? Maybe it was his imagination. He wasn't sure. He kept turning to look over his shoulder as he heard various sounds and then paused to consider if each noise was real or just his mind playing tricks on him.

Saturday morning was rough. Daniel had not slept well knowing he was alone in such a big building. Even though he knew the doors were secured and the building was safe, Daniel still felt uneasy. In a residence hall, there is generally some sort of noise most of the time. Over the course of the semester, residents become accustomed to it and can naturally sleep through it. Last night, it was the actual lack of background noise that had disrupted Daniel's sleep. He tried to sleep late to make up for the time he spent awake tossing and turning but soon realized that was a futile effort. He crawled out of bed and opened his curtains. This proved to be a mistake as the sun reflecting off the fallen snow blinded Daniel. He made a pot of coffee, fixed some cinnamon rolls, and settled in for a day of studying.

Despite the internet still not being restored, Daniel had some textbook reading he could do and class notes to review. After reading the first chapter he had been assigned, Daniel needed a break. Normally he would visit with some friends in the residence hall. Of course, that was not an option today. He decided to make a round of the residence hall and stretch his legs.

As he walked the silent halls, Daniel considered how long it had actually been since he spent any time in silence and solitude. He sometimes studied in the library, but there were always other people around. When he studied in his room, he usually had the television on for background noise. Even when traveling long distances by car, he always had the radio on. How long had it really been since he had been alone with his thoughts?

Throughout the rest of the duty weekend, Daniel thought about his upcoming graduation, which was just two semesters away. What kinds of positions would he apply for? How far would he be willing to move for the right job? Would it be better to continue his education and go to graduate school before entering the workforce? He had some important decisions ahead of him, and it really wouldn't be that long until he had to start making some of them.

During an afternoon study break, Daniel updated the bulletin boards in the building. One of the flyers was for an upcoming event at the campus ministry Brandon attended. Brandon was a good friend, and Daniel had begun going to church after Brandon had invited him. He had met some really good people there and learned a lot. Daniel's thoughts turned to what he really believed about God.

Really, my only thoughts about heaven and hell were in the cartoons I watched growing up, he thought. One of the characters would have a version of himself on each shoulder, one an angel wearing a robe with a halo and the other a devil dressed in red with horns, a tail, and carrying a pitchfork. But what really happens when you die? When Daniel had been at funerals, people always said the deceased was in a better place now. But how much did he really know about heaven?

He considered this, thinking how no one had ever gone into detail with him about what it is really like in heaven.

And who gets to go? At church, he heard all kinds of Bible stories about characters messed up in various ways. He had heard stories growing up about times God acted in epic ways and characters had lived out their faith in dynamic ways but had never really thought about whether he believed they were true. Going to church right now was more of a social outlet. He figured everyone at church is supposed to be a nice person, so why not go there to meet new people? But if the stories he had heard there were true, it would be revolutionary. It would mean that there is so much more to the Christian life than just being a nice person.

It was actually very comforting to think about how messed up everyone is. The characters that God used in the Bible certainly didn't always get it right. The preacher talked about the struggles we face today and how God loves us no matter how often we fail. Then in some of the small groups, Daniel had heard different people share ways they were struggling. For so long, he had thought he was alone in how he felt. He could be a procrastinator. He wasn't always honest with people. He wasn't sure where he wanted to live or exactly what he wanted to do after graduation. But it seemed that a lot of people shared these struggles.

Daniel thought about how hard he tried to look like he had everything together. He needed to present a strong image for his residents. He needed to appear confident or his friends might think he was weak. He wanted to appear decisive in front of his girlfriend. But then the openness of Jesus's disciples came to mind. A recent sermon he heard explored how we know the stories about all the times the disciples failed or made poor decisions. The pastor gave lots of examples. They were on a boat with Jesus during a storm and were terrified. At one point, Peter had denied even knowing Jesus. The point of the sermon was that the disciples put Jesus ahead of their own image. We know about their failures because they shared these stories with us through the four gospels.

Daniel thought about how tired he was. But I'm not physically tired, he thought. I'm so tired of looking like I have everything together. It would be so nice to have what the disciples had. They were so committed to Jesus that they were willing to share their failures and insecurities with each other, and with the world. The pastor had shared that you would want to be sure that anyone you open up to can be trusted. If I allow myself to be vulnerable, Daniel thought, I definitely don't want my weaknesses spread around through the gossip chain. But it would sure be nice to have some friendships with people I don't have to pretend around.

Daniel considered these things on and off the rest of the weekend. He might even have a conversation with Brandon about these matters that consumed his thoughts. Brandon seemed like someone that Daniel could trust. He might be able to share with some of the guys in the small group on Sunday morning too. As bored as Daniel was at times over the weekend, he was really glad things turned out the way they did. Having this quiet time to himself had really allowed him to think through some things that were weighing on him.

On Sunday evening, residents started returning from the break. Daniel enjoyed the return of his friends to the formerly lifeless residence hall. But even as Cordell Hall came back to life, he made a commitment to himself to spend some time in solitude each week so he could consider the direction of his life and the things he was learning in church.

Scripture

Psalm 119:9-16

How can a young person stay on the path of purity?
By living according to your word.
I seek you with all my heart;
do not let me stray from your commands.
I have hidden your word in my heart
that I might not sin against you.
Praise be to you, Lord;
teach me your decrees.
With my lips I recount
all the laws that come from your mouth.
I rejoice in following your statutes
as one rejoices in great riches.
I meditate on your precepts
and consider your ways.
I delight in your decrees;
I will not neglect your word.

Luke 5:15

Yet the news about him spread all the more, so that crowds of people came to hear him and to be healed of their sicknesses. But Jesus often withdrew to lonely places and prayed.

Matthew 14:13-14

When Jesus heard what had happened, he withdrew by boat privately to a solitary place. Hearing of this, the crowds followed him on foot from the towns. When Jesus landed and saw a large crowd, he had compassion on them and healed their sick.

Matthew 14:22-24

Immediately Jesus made the disciples get into the boat and go on ahead of him to the other side, while he dismissed the crowd. After he had dismissed them, he went up on a mountainside by himself to pray. Later that night, he was there alone, and the boat was already a considerable distance from land, buffeted by the waves because the wind was against it.

Questions

1. In the story, Daniel finds himself alone, separated from people both physically and through outlets like social media. Tell about a time that you spent in solitude, separated from other people. Did you isolate yourself on purpose or were you isolated due to circumstances outside your control? How did being cut off make you feel?

2. Sometimes we choose to isolate ourselves. Perhaps it is to consider an important decision. It may just be a place where you can take a break from the busyness of life. When was the most recent time you spent in solitude? What is a place that you like to go when you need to be alone with your thoughts? Why did you choose that particular place?

3. The scripture readings from Matthew and Luke describe multiple times Jesus withdrew to solitary places to pray. Were you surprised to read that Jesus took time to withdraw and spend time in prayer? What can we learn from the way Jesus modeled this behavior?

4. The scripture reading from Psalm 119 mentions meditating. What do you think of when you hear the word meditate? How much of a priority do you think the church today puts on spending time in solitude to spend on our spiritual well-being? Why do you think that is? How much of a priority is taking time for yourself to spend in solitude? If it is not a current priority, where could you find places in your schedule

to incorporate time to be alone with God, whether reading scripture, praying, or just listening for His voice?

5. Daniel's time of solitude allowed him to really consider what he believed about God in a much deeper way than he had previously done. Where would you like to go deeper in your understanding of God? In what ways would you like to know Him better?

6. Spending time in solitude can be useful in a variety of ways. Time could be spent in prayer, enjoying the beauty of nature, reading and memorizing scripture, or listening for God's voice. Which, if any, of these have you tried? What was the experience like? In times that we simply listen for God's voice, how can we keep our minds from wandering away from God and moving towards our to-do lists? What helps you to stay focused during time you have set aside to spend with God?

Challenge for the Week

Consider how you answered the last discussion question. Commit to spending time alone each week for a month reading over this week's scripture verses. After reading over the scripture, take five minutes to pray or just listen for God's voice. This may feel awkward if it is something new for you, but try to remain in silence for the full five minutes. At the end of the month, take time to think about how you felt during your time in solitude.

CHAPTER 5

Christmas Break

Brandon was excited to be home for Christmas. He had a fantastic time celebrating with his family, but he was especially looking forward to catching up with his friends from high school. Of course, he followed his friends on social media and also kept in touch through texting, emails, and video chats. But there was nothing like seeing each other and sharing stories firsthand.

He parked his car at Jake's Diner, the place he and his friends had spent so many afternoons following school. Just seeing the building made Brandon smile. He thought the place had the best hamburgers in town. It seemed like Jake's Diner had been around forever. His parents talked about going there when they were dating. The place had a 1950s theme. The outside of the building was a bright red and yellow, and the inside had a jukebox with all the hits from the '50s. In addition to the tables and booths, there was a counter where customers could sit.

Brandon went inside and found Jessica, Jacob, and Rob already seated at their favorite booth. After giving everyone hugs, they all sat down. When their server approached, they didn't even need a menu. Everyone had their favorite item and they went ahead and ordered their meal.

They immediately started sharing stories about their first semester. As the day went on, they talked about different people they had met, what life was like living on campus, and adapting to life away from home. Hearing about each other's experiences was so much better than reading posts on social media or sharing through text messages.

"That first week was crazy," Rob said. "Not knowing anybody, barely remembering my way to class."

"And nobody to wake you up in the morning! You were always late to first period last year," Jessica said as she laughed.

"I know!" Rob agreed. "I was late to my history class so often, I almost started losing points on my final grade."

"So, what's the craziest thing that has happened to each of you so far?" Jacob asked.

"You won't believe it, but I joined a swing dance club," Rob said.

"You're joking," Brandon said, half as a statement and halfway questioning Rob.

"No joke," Rob said. "A couple of guys in my dorm were in it last year and said it was really fun. Plus, there are always more girls than guys. Since I wasn't dating anyone, I figured why not go where the odds would be in my favor."

"The truth comes out," Jessica said.

Rob shared more about swing dancing. He had, in fact, started dating someone he met in the club. Brandon was up next.

"The craziest thing would have to be this one night a bunch of us played capture the flag, but with Super Soakers." Brandon said.

Brandon went on to tell how they played late at night around a local church. While they usually had the church's permission, one night they decided to play and figured it wouldn't hurt to just go on and play. What they didn't know was that the church was hosting visiting missionaries who were asleep in the building.

Brandon continued telling the story. "So, the missionaries must have called someone with the church. The pastor comes rolling in at midnight like he's racing in the Daytona 500. He had on a bath robe over a T-shirt and flannel pants and his hair was all crazy and standing up. He wanted to know what we thought we were doing." Brandon was laughing so hard he was almost crying. "We were scared out of our minds. I'm sure those poor missionaries thought we were coming for them."

Jessica was next and shared about serving in student government. She talked about a tree that was a fixture on campus. But a planned addition to the football stadium put the tree's future in jeopardy.

"In order to draw attention to their cause, a bunch of students started chaining themselves to the tree during every home game! There were news crews from all over the state shooting video and interviewing the protesters. Of course, the powers-that-be didn't want to look like they were in favor of killing a piece of our history, so they asked us in the student senate to look into it."

"What did you do?" Jacob asked.

"What could we do?" Jessica replied. "They were the ones paid to deal with this sort of thing. We represent the student body but really don't have a lot of actual authority. And when we talked about it, the majority of us backed finding a way to preserve the tree. We weren't even on the administration's side. What we are trying to do now is see if the addition can move forward at a different part of the stadium or in a way that doesn't require the tree to be removed."

"Nice," said Brandon. "That would be a win-win. What about you Jacob? You asked us about our wild and crazy lives. What's your story?

"Where do I start?" Jacob asked. "Here's a good one. I got invited to this party at a house a few blocks off campus. A bunch of guys from my apartment building were there. Someone brought a keg and we were all hanging out in the backyard. I guess we got the music too loud because next thing I know I see blue lights in the driveway. I bet over half of us were under 21 and scared for our lives! The guy I rode with told me to meet him at the car or I'd have to find my own way back to campus." Jacob went on to tell how they were able to get away and how some of the guys had to run through people's backyards as they tried to get back to campus by foot. It was a funny story, but it did shock Brandon a bit.

Jacob went on to tell several stories about other parties he had attended. Brandon couldn't help but feel judgmental. There was nothing wrong with going to a party, but the parties Jacob described were wilder than anything Brandon had ever seen. Brandon also noticed Jacob cursing often as he spoke about his first semester of college. Brandon knew that his language was not exactly perfect. Neither was Jessica or Rob's. But there was a difference with Jacob.

Rob laughed as Jacob finished another story. "I bet that makes it hard to get out of bed on Sunday morning."

"You have no idea," Jacob said. "I usually don't get up until at least 11. I run out for food before the NFL games get started, or I just meet up with some folks at a sports bar and watch the games there."

"Don't you miss going to church?" Brandon asked. "You were always there back in high school. I know it has been a big help for me in making new friends."

Jessica and Rob had found church homes at their respective schools and shared how they had also made some good friends. Jacob shrugged and told them there was always something fun happening on Saturday night. Even if he stayed at his apartment complex, someone was always having people over until the middle of the night.

Rob asked Jacob if he didn't miss the fellowship and just being in church. Jacob replied that church had always been more of a social thing for him. He further explained that he had made great friends in his classes and in his apartment complex. Jacob felt he was getting his need for community met with his new friends.

Jessica asked about having a support system. Before leaving for college, they had all opened up about how living away from home for the first time would be scary. Nobody really shared this on their social media accounts, though. They primarily posted pictures of them having fun or funny memes and viral videos. Jessica said that keeping in touch had been a source of encouragement, but she discovered that finding a local church had been an even greater source of support. An added bonus was meeting people who shared a common faith.

Jacob responded by saying he felt like he was a good person. He had learned all about living with honesty and integrity in high school and in church. Continuing to invest time in church didn't seem like it should be a priority anymore. Jacob's roommates and neighbors had all become really good friends. If he ever felt homesick, he could always find someone to hang out with and take his mind off his homesickness.

The conversation eventually shifted to other topics. The friends spent several hours catching up and realized how busy they had all been during their first semester of college. Even though they had kept in touch, their communication had become more spread out as the semester had gone on. It wasn't that they weren't interested in keeping in touch. Life just seemed to get busy with schoolwork, meeting and getting to know new people, and figuring out which campus organizations they would enjoy joining. As they were leaving, everyone agreed to try and see each other a few more times before returning to school for spring semester.

As Brandon drove home, he couldn't help but dwell on the changes he observed in Jacob. Maybe it was nothing. Lots of people go through a wild phase when they first experience freedom away from home. However, Brandon's concern for Jacob's spiritual health stayed on his mind the rest of the day.

Being raised in church, he always just assumed Jessica, Jacob, and Rob were all Christians. As he looked back, however, he realized they had never really had any deep conversations about their faith. And I know other Christians that don't go to church, Brandon thought. It doesn't mean Jacob isn't a Christian just because he chose not to find a church to attend. But some of the things he said raised some serious questions for Brandon. Jacob had not really talked about his faith during their lunch. He only spoke about the social aspects of church. And that need was being met through his friends at his apartments. Jacob had always been a nice guy and a lot of fun when they were part of their church's high school youth group. But, Brandon thought, I know a lot of nice guys who are not Christians.

That night, as Brandon prepared for bed, he decided that he would be more deliberate about seeing how his friends are growing spiritually as well as where they might be struggling. He thought these conversations might be awkward at first. This was not something he and his friends ever really discussed. But he knew he appreciated it when people asked how he was doing and Brandon wanted to do the same for his friends.

He would also take time to pray for his friends. Brandon didn't know how God worked through prayer, but he knew people in both his hometown and on campus that were not Christians. They needed prayer, and Brandon would also pray that God would give him opportunities to share his faith. He would begin this tonight, and Jacob would be the first person he would lift up in prayer.

Scripture

Matthew 18:15-20

If your brother or sister sins, go and point out their fault, just between the two of you. If they listen to you, you have won them over. But if they will not listen, take one or two others along, so that 'every matter may be established by the testimony of two or three witnesses.' If they still refuse to listen, tell it to the church; and if they refuse to listen even to the church, treat them as you would a pagan or a tax collector.

Truly I tell you, whatever you bind on earth will be bound in heaven, and whatever you loose on earth will be loosed in heaven.

Again, truly I tell you that if two of you on earth agree about anything they ask for, it will be done for them by my Father in heaven. For where two or three gather in my name, there am I with them.

Ephesians 5:1-20

Follow God's example, therefore, as dearly loved children and walk in the way of love, just as Christ loved us and gave himself up for us as a fragrant offering and sacrifice to God.

But among you there must not be even a hint of sexual immorality, or of any kind of impurity, or of greed, because these are improper for God's holy people. Nor should there be obscenity, foolish talk or coarse joking, which are out of place, but rather thanksgiving. For of this you can be sure: No immoral, impure or greedy person—such a person is an idolater—has any inheritance in the kingdom of Christ and of God. Let no one deceive you with empty words, for because of such things God's wrath comes on those who are disobedient. Therefore, do not be partners with them.

For you were once darkness, but now you are light in the Lord. Live as children of light (for the fruit of the light consists in all goodness, righteousness and truth) and find out what pleases the Lord. Have nothing to do with the fruitless deeds of darkness, but rather expose them. It is shameful even to mention what the disobedient do in secret. But everything exposed by the light becomes visible—and everything that is illuminated becomes a light. This is why it is said:

"Wake up, sleeper,
rise from the dead,
and Christ will shine on you."

Be very careful, then, how you live—not as unwise but as wise, making the most of every opportunity, because the days are evil. Therefore, do not be foolish, but understand what the Lord's will is. Do not get drunk on wine, which leads to debauchery. Instead, be filled with the Spirit, speaking to one another with psalms, hymns, and songs from the Spirit. Sing and make music from your heart to the Lord, always giving thanks to God the Father for everything, in the name of our Lord Jesus Christ.

Colossians 4:2-6

Devote yourselves to prayer, being watchful and thankful. And pray for us, too, that God may open a door for our message, so that we may proclaim the mystery of Christ, for which I am in chains. Pray that I may proclaim it clearly, as I should. Be wise in the way you act toward outsiders; make the most of every opportunity. Let your conversation be always full of grace, seasoned with salt, so that you may know how to answer everyone.

Proverbs 27:6

Wounds from a friend can be trusted,
but an enemy multiplies kisses.

Questions

1. What are some of the biggest changes in your life since graduating from high school?

2. The first semester of college brings a lot of new experiences. What are some ways you have handled being in a new situation where you may feel anxious?

3. As you read the scripture passages, consider the following:

    a. Matthew 18:15–20 – We will meet people with differing tastes and opinions throughout life. Differences among Christians may include the types of music and entertainment we enjoy, eating and drinking habits, and the way we vote. How would you go about deciding whether something may just be a difference of opinion or something that you should discuss with your friend? In general, people tend to avoid conflict. How would you handle a situation where a Christian friend was caught in a sinful behavior? How would you respond if one or two of your friends approached you about a possible sinful behavior in your life?

    b. Ephesians 5:1–20 – How does this passage say that Christ-followers are to behave? What actions should be avoided? If a person's place in heaven is secured after he or she accepts Christ, then why does it matter how we conduct ourselves? There is an expression that says "You may be the only Bible some people ever read." What does that mean to you?

    c. Colossians 4:2-6 – What are some ways that we can show wisdom in how we conduct ourselves around non-Christians? In this passage, Paul asks for prayer for himself and Timothy. What are some ways we can both support and seek support from trusted friends? As you answer, consider how much is appropriate to share with different groups in your lives (classmates, acquaintances, close friends, family).

    d. Proverbs 27:6 – How do you interpret this verse? Consider if you have anyone you trust enough to take seriously and listen if they were to confront you about a possible sin in your life. Consider whether there is anyone you are close enough to that you could go to if they were behaving in an irresponsible way.

4. One of the ways Brandon kept up with his friends was through social media, but there was still a lot he didn't know about their lives. How do you think people usually present themselves on social media? Why do you think that is? Think about the types of posts you see on social media. Which types of posts do you enjoy the most? Which types annoy you?

5. In the scripture reading, how are Christians encouraged to conduct themselves? How can the people we surround ourselves with help or hinder

our efforts to conduct ourselves in a way that honors Christ?

6. Brandon is concerned about how Jacob has changed since they last saw each other. What would you do if you were in Brandon's position? Much of the scripture for this chapter is based on how Christians can hold each other accountable. After the conversation the friends had in this chapter, Brandon is no longer sure that Jacob is a Christian. Does this change your opinion of how you think Brandon should handle the situation? Why or why not?

Challenge for the Week

Think of someone you have lost contact with. Take time this week to reach out to this person and have a conversation. Also commit to pray for this person over the next week.

CHAPTER 6

When You Don't Quite Fit In

Brandon was glad to see everyone at the first Campus Christian Assembly gathering of the semester. Tuesday night worship was one of his favorite parts of the week, and when it was over, people started making plans for the weekend. One group was going to a lock-in at the campus fitness center. Everything there would be open all night for students to enjoy. There would be a rock-climbing wall, open basketball and racquetball courts, as well as one gym having a movie projector set up. Even the swimming pool would be open all night. As Brandon talked to some of his closer friends, they decided to go bowling and then to meet everyone else a little later at the lock-in.

As everyone discussed their plans, Brandon noticed Ethan standing just off to the side of the group that was going early to the lock-in. He was a nice guy but could be awkward in social situations. Sometimes this made finding things to talk about with Ethan difficult. One of his favorite hobbies was building models. It didn't matter if it was model cars, airplanes, or ships. Ethan loved to talk about his hobby, but sometimes people got tired of hearing about his models. As Ethan stood by the group, the conversation continued.

"Eight o'clock seems to work for everyone. Where do we want to meet?" Scott asked.

"Why don't we just meet here?" Keith asked. "It's not that far and we could just walk down together."

"We wouldn't have to worry about finding each other. That place is going to be packed." Beth added.

"I bet it will be tough to do any of the activities until the crowd thins out," Maria said. "Even with as many things as will be going on, the lines are going to be long."

"Maybe we could start out in the pool, or see what movie is playing in the gym so we don't have to wait," Ethan suggested.

"I say we just check it out when we get there and decide from there," Alex said.

"Yeah, that's a good idea," Beth agreed. "We don't have to go in a certain order. We'll just play it by ear."

Keith said, "Some of my neighbors on campus are planning to play basketball when they get there. They will be there early to get a court, so that's always an option."

Scott laughed. "Then we'll be all sweaty and nasty the rest of the night."

"That's what the pool is for!" Maria exclaimed.

Alex said, "All I know is I'm going to the top of that rock climbing wall before the night is done."

"That's too high for me," Ethan said. "I'll cheer for you from down on the ground."

"Are any of the courts going to be set up for volleyball?" Scott asked.

"I would think so," Beth answered. "There are so many courts in that place that surely there will be somewhere to play volleyball."

Scott said, "It would be great for us to get a few games in, especially before the intramural tournament starts next month. Everyone remember to get me their T-shirt sizes so I can turn them in with our registration form."

Ethan spoke up. "I didn't know we were doing a tournament."

"Oh, sorry," Keith said. "You didn't sign up for flag football or any of the intramurals around homecoming. I just didn't think you played sports."

"I like to play more for fun," Ethan said.

"Well, I've got to go. Need to study for my statistics quiz tomorrow," Alex said. "But it sounds like we're set. I'll see everyone Friday at eight."

Everyone said bye to Alex as he left. The group continued discussing the lock-in. Brandon and Austin had finished working out their plans to go bowling and joined the group. As they listened to the conversation, Brandon noticed that as they spoke about which events at the lock-in they were most excited to do, none of them responded to Ethan or made a point to include him in the conversation. Brandon observed that while no one excluded Ethan, they didn't go out of their way to include him either. What upset Brandon most was that this group was mostly made up of students in leadership positions. There were a few that were in the praise band and others that were in charge of planning worship and fellowship events. They weren't his closest friends, but they were people that Brandon respected. It was a tremendous shock to Brandon to see them finish up making plans without paying any attention to Ethan.

Brandon leaned over to Austin and spoke quietly. "Should we invite Ethan to go with us?"

"It sounds like he is going with the group early to the lock-in," Austin replied.

"He is, but no one is talking to him." Brandon said.

"I guess it wouldn't hurt. Either way, we'll all be there eventually." Austin then spoke to the entire group. "We'll look for you when we get there. A few of us are going bowling before we go to the lock-in."

Brandon followed by saying, "If anyone wants to bowl first, we'll be at Extreme Bowling at seven."

Several members of the other group thanked them for the offer but said they were going to spend the whole night at the lock-in. They all talked for a few more minutes about which events they were most excited about. Eventually, people started leaving for the night.

"Ethan," Brandon said, "you're welcome to join us if you want."

"Thanks," Ethan replied, "I haven't been bowling in over a year. I think I'll meet you there."

Brandon and Austin said their goodbyes and began their walk back to Cordell Hall.

"You just put another jewel in your crown in heaven." Austin laughed.

"Ethan can definitely wear out his welcome, but at least he got an actual invitation from us," Brandon replied. "Honestly, he gets on my nerves, but I figure we have a big enough group bowling that we can handle him."

"True," Austin said. "And we didn't see him much at the end of last semester. I think my tolerance meter is pretty high right now."

Brandon laughed as they approached the front steps of Cordell Hall.

Scripture

Matthew 12:46-50

While Jesus was still talking to the crowd, his mother and brothers stood outside, wanting to speak to him. Someone told him, "Your mother and brothers are standing outside, wanting to speak to you."

He replied to him, "Who is my mother, and who are my brothers?" Pointing to his disciples, he said, "Here are my mother and my brothers. For whoever does the will of my Father in heaven is my brother and sister and mother."

Matthew 22:34-40

Hearing that Jesus had silenced the Sadducees, the Pharisees got together. One of them, an expert in the law, tested him with this question: "Teacher, which is the greatest commandment in the Law?"

Jesus replied: "'Love the Lord your God with all your heart and with all your soul and with all your mind.' This is the first and greatest commandment. And the second is like it: 'Love your neighbor as yourself.' All the Law and the Prophets hang on these two commandments."

Questions

1. Read the scripture from Matthew chapter 12. Who does Jesus say is His family? If you apply this scripture to your life, who is your family?

2. The scripture from Matthew chapter 22 was also part of chapter 3. It has what many people call the Golden Rule, which is also applicable to this chapter. Reflect on your previous conversation. What do you think most people believe it means to love your neighbor as yourself? Consider all the ways that you wish people would treat you. Consider some recent times that you don't feel you were treated fairly or with kindness. Based on your reflection, what would it look like in action if we truly lived this out?

3. There are two groups in the story, one that is going to the lock-in early and another that is bowling first. How did the two groups treat Ethan differently?

4. Brandon and Austin acknowledged that Ethan gets on their nerves. Imagine you are in their position. As you go through the different events of your semester, how would you determine how often to invite a person who is not a close friend to those events? How would your answer change when planning an official Campus Christian Assembly event compared to just getting some friends together?

5. Building a community requires creating a welcoming environment. What responsibility do we as individuals have in plugging into a new group to meet new people? What are some practical ways

you can help create a welcoming environment in the student organizations to which you belong? Whereas extroverts are more outgoing, introverts are quieter and may appreciate being included without becoming the center of attention. How could you be welcoming to more introverted friends without making them uncomfortable?

Challenge for the Week

Look back at your first few weeks in college. What were some of the things you appreciated that made you feel welcome? What did you wish someone had done to make you feel welcome? As you go through this week, commit to seek out opportunities to make those around you feel welcome.

CHAPTER 7

Spring Break

Spring break had arrived! Brandon was thrilled to have a week off from his classes. He was, however, a bit shocked at where he found himself. When he started college last fall, spring break was one of the things he was most looking forward to. He had wondered if he would find himself at a popular beach, an amusement park, or possibly a music festival. Instead of a party destination, however, Brandon found himself on a service trip to a town barely a day's drive from campus.

Although it wasn't where Brandon expected to be, he was glad to be on this trip. Most of the people he had grown close to were also there. Even Lauren, a friend he had gone to high school with, was on the trip. He also appreciated the variety of ways he could serve. The group had projects throughout the community they were visiting. Among them were opportunities to serve at a soup kitchen, lead worship and Bible studies at a local park, paint houses for low-income families, and sort items at a distribution warehouse. With projects spread throughout the day, it gave the students a chance to serve at multiple places.

Brandon, Tracy, Lauren, Ryan, Derrek, and Parker were on a team working at the distribution warehouse. Donated goods from across the region were shipped to the warehouse. From there, items were grouped, boxed up, and sent out to shelters for homeless families. Some boxes were stocked with nonperishable food items including canned goods and dry pasta. Others were stocked with personal items such as soap, shampoo, and toothpaste.

The students arrived and were given a tour of the warehouse. The building was enormous. Palates of boxes filled with donated items to be sorted rose like skyscrapers. There were cargo bays where tractor trailers could drop off donations and pick up sorted items to get back out into communities.

Next, they were introduced to the warehouse staff with whom they would be working. Everyone chatted together for a few minutes. Then, the staff showed the students the area where they would be working.

Rita, one of the warehouse employees, explained the process. "We'll be working with you at this long table. If your group wants to work on the side with the stacks of boxes, that would be great. Each box has come from a donation center and could contain a combination of canned goods, clothing, or personal items like shampoo and toothpaste. What your group will do is separate out these items. My team will be on the other side of the table repackaging everything according to whether it is clothing, canned goods, or personal hygiene items. Then the goods can go out to shelters depending on the individual needs of each shelter."

"Sounds simple enough," said Parker.

"It's not hard," Rita agreed. "One other thing. With clothing, if an item is too ragged to really be useful, just toss it to the side. Anything we can't use will get thrown out."

Ryan said, "That seems wasteful. Wouldn't it be better that someone gets a damaged coat or pair of pants than not get anything at all?"

Perry, another employee, spoke up. "One thing we are trying to do is respect the dignity of the people who get these items. A lot of people use places like this to clean out their closets, and that can be a good thing. The downside is when we get items that are not really fit to be worn anymore. The people that will get this stuff are all unique individuals with a sense of dignity. We try to honor that."

"And as you can see," Rita said, motioning to the sea of boxes around them, "there is no shortage of clothing to be sorted. We have plenty to get out, but what we really need are more hands to help organize everything. That's why we're glad to have you here."

"Well, let's get to it then," Tracy said.

Before they moved to the table to begin, Brandon said, "One thing we would like to do is periodically rotate some of us out to pray over the goods being sorted, as well as for the volunteers and employees that worked at the various donation centers and warehouses."

For safety reasons, students would work in pairs for this. Brandon and Lauren took the first shift. While walking throughout the warehouse, they additionally prayed that enough donations would come so that each shelter would get everything it needed. Because the group had gotten a late start, Brandon and Lauren would finish the morning and trade out sorting boxes with two other students after lunch.

Everyone was eager to get started and quickly began going through boxes. It felt very chaotic at first. Soon, however, the students found a rhythm in sorting boxes so they were not all on top of each other. Once in this rhythm, they were able to move at a rapid pace.

During their lunch break, the students sat outside to get some fresh air.

"We are really moving those boxes," Ryan said.

"Yeah," Tracy agreed. "If we keep up this pace, I'm going to break a sweat soon."

Derrick laughed. "Some of the staff already are. We are crushing it with how much we are getting done."

Parker said, "Just think of how much bigger the shipment is going to be at the end of the week. I bet the people at the shelters won't know what to think."

"They will definitely be in for a shock," Brandon added. "You wouldn't believe how deep this warehouse is. Lauren and I have been going all morning and I don't know if we've even covered a third of it yet."

Derrick thought about what Brandon said. "Maybe after lunch, we should have prayer teams going for the rest of the day. That way we would be sure to cover everything."

Lauren had been listening to the conversation. "How are the employees? Have you gotten to know any of them?"

"Not really," Ryan answered. "We've really been focused on getting through as many boxes as possible."

"Sure, but what if the mission is not the mission?" Lauren asked.

"Huh?" Tracy replied, sounding confused. "I'm not sure what you mean."

"Well, I just think we are missing a big opportunity,"

Lauren explained. We are praying for everyone that donates and receives these items, as well as the employees and volunteers. We are working hard to get a lot done this week. But I think we may be missing a chance to serve the staff right here."

"How so?" Parker asked. "We have been busting our tails."

"I'm sure you have. But it might be worth taking some time to get to know the people we are working with. This can be physically demanding work, and the staff here don't get to see those moments when a family receives the items being sorted here."

"There hasn't been a lot of conversation," Parker acknowledged.

The students continued to talk and made a decision. They would work hard but not at such a grueling pace. They would also make more of an effort to get to know the staff they were serving with. And rather than have students walking throughout the warehouse and praying over every part of the process, the group would reserve time to do that before and after their work day began. Then, during the day, they would all be engaged in sorting items. This would allow them to continue being productive in the work to be done but also allow time to connect with the warehouse staff.

It turned out that Lauren was right. As everyone continued working in the afternoon, the students struck up conversations with the employees. The students really enjoyed getting to know everyone. There was a radio tuned into a classic rock station, and at times everyone would sing along with a familiar song. That led into some of Brandon's group suggesting they teach the warehouse staff some praise songs they knew.

As the week went on, much was accomplished at the warehouse. A lot of donated items were sorted and ready to go to shelters. The staff had been encouraged and seemed to really enjoy themselves. And thanks to Lauren, the students had learned a valuable lesson.

Sometimes the mission is not the mission.

Scripture

Luke 10:38-42

As Jesus and his disciples were on their way, he came to a village where a woman named Martha opened her home to him. She had a sister called Mary, who sat at the Lord's feet listening to what he said. But Martha was distracted by all the preparations that had to be made. She came to him and asked, "Lord, don't you care that my sister has left me to do the work by myself? Tell her to help me!"

"Martha, Martha," the Lord answered, "you are worried and upset about many things, but few things are needed—or indeed only one. Mary has chosen what is better, and it will not be taken away from her."

1 Peter 4:9-11

Offer hospitality to one another without grumbling. Each of you should use whatever gift you have received to serve others, as faithful stewards of God's grace in its various forms. If anyone speaks, they should do so as one who speaks the very words of God. If anyone serves, they should do so with the strength God provides, so that in all things God may be praised through Jesus Christ. To him be the glory and the power for ever and ever. Amen.

Questions

1. Think of a time you had an opportunity to volunteer or serve. What about it was meaningful for you?

2. Read the scripture from Luke. How did Martha and Mary behave differently while Jesus was visiting with them? Why was Martha upset with Mary? What do you think Jesus meant by what he said to Martha?

3. How can this scripture relate to the story you just read?

4. Everyone except Lauren was primarily focused on sorting the donated items. Was there anything inherently wrong with their focus?

5. Some service opportunities such as home repairs or food distribution allow us to see the results of our works. Others such as backyard Bible clubs are about building relationships. We may not see immediate results from those, but we trust that God would be at work to change lives. Both types of service are important. What types of service opportunities do you find most rewarding? Why?

6. The scripture from 1 Peter discusses offering hospitality. Where is a place that you feel like you were shown excellent hospitality? What was it that made you feel so welcome and appreciated? Now think about a church or campus ministry to which you belong. In what ways do you see hospitality being offered? What are some strategies we might use in our lives so that we do not miss an opportunity to serve?

Challenge for the Week

The previous lesson's challenge included thinking of people around you who have the gift of hospitality. This week, reach out to someone who really made you feel welcome and thank them. The person you thank may not feel they did anything special. Point out how important the gift of hospitality is and how you saw it through their actions.

CHAPTER 8

Goodbye Winter, Hello Spring!

Campus seemed to come alive! Spring fever was in the air as students said goodbye to winter and embraced a welcome rise in temperatures. It was also the week leading up to Easter, so there would be a short week of classes. With the arrival of warmer weather, Chris had taken the top off his jeep. Chris, Austin, Amanda and Hannah were cruising campus and enjoying the sunshine and fresh air.

"Turn here, I want to go by Ellington Apartments," Amanda said to Chris.

"Why?" Chris asked. "The road just dead ends once you get to Ellington."

"You'll see." Amanda laughed.

Chris turned the jeep toward Ellington Apartments, which happened to be where many of the male athletes lived. As he approached the apartments, everyone noticed the basketball court and sand volleyball court were both being used. Chris rolled his eyes as he realized why Amanda wanted to come this way.

"You just want to check out the guys!" he exclaimed.

Amanda burst into laughter. "They're so hot!"

"You're awful," Chris said jokingly.

"Slow down!" Amanda said. "I want to see if this guy in my English Comp class is out there. I think he broke up with his girlfriend."

Chris slowed down to a turtle's pace as the jeep rounded the front of the basketball court. "Well, this isn't obvious at all," Austin said sarcastically.

"I don't see him." Amanda sighed with disappointment in her voice. Then she perked up. "But there's a guy that sits near me in my sociology class! Wow, he's in better shape than I realized!"

Amanda waved at him. He saw her and waved back.

"Are we done here?" Austin asked.

"Hey, you said you wanted to go for a ride in the jeep and enjoy the warm day," Amanda said. "You didn't say anything about where you wanted to go. Just relax. This is me enjoying the day and the scenery."

Austin protested. "When I said that, this was not what I had in mind."

"Well," Chris said, "if you get to check out the guys here, then I'm making the Lucy Loop next!"

"Fine, if we have to," Hannah said.

"Hey, fair is fair," Chris said as he turned his jeep around in front of the guys playing volleyball.

Austin had heard the guys in the residence hall talk about the Lucy Loop ever since the spring semester had started. Lucille Taylor Hall was one of the nicer female residence halls on campus. It had a large grassy area both in front and behind it. The Lucy Loop was what the men on campus called driving by to see how many women were out sunbathing when warm weather arrived.

Chris was not disappointed as he spotted a group of sunbathers while entering the Lucy Loop. "Now we're talking!"

Chris slowed up and Amanda called him out, saying sarcastically "Take your time. Don't want you to miss anything."

"Hey!" Chris exclaimed, faking injury. "I'm doing this for you. There are speed bumps in front of Lucy. I don't want to knock everyone out of their seats. And you're the one who made a big deal about enjoying the scenery at Ellington."

"Well," Hannah said, "if everyone is happy now, can we go get lunch? I'm starving."

Everyone laughed as Chris left campus going towards the Tiger's Den, a popular sandwich shop beside campus. A spring shower appeared to be approaching, so the guys put the top back on the jeep. Amanda and Hannah went on inside the Tiger's Den. Hannah thought about the drive by the men's residence hall.

Hannah spoke up. "You know, I've always tried to value people by their character, but those were some of the fittest men I've ever seen. They were definitely in better shape than any of the guys I dated in high school."

Amanda laughed. "I know, right?"

"But you do want more than just a guy with chiseled abs, don't you?"

"Of course. Well, eventually. Isn't this the time in our lives we're supposed to just be dating and having fun? I don't even know what I want yet. We're just freshmen, you know?"

"I know. I also think dating different people is a good way to figure out what we want." Hannah paused and then continued. "And what we don't want. You know that good looks won't last forever."

"That's why I've got to enjoy them now. And I've got forever to settle down. And settling down is not even on my radar right now."

"You're a mess," Hannah said as she and Amanda approached the counter to place their orders.

Hannah knew there were more important things than looks, but she still thought about the guys she saw at Ellington for a big part of the afternoon. She knew she wanted a guy with a good heart, but Amanda had stirred up an internal conflict within her. This was supposed to be a time to date different people and figure out what she wants in the person she eventually marries. And attraction has to be part of the equation, doesn't it? God wouldn't give us these feelings of attraction unless they mattered, would He? And if marriage and a family are both years away, why not have a little fun now? These questions made Hannah wonder whether she was taking the idea of dating too seriously. Of course, choosing a partner to marry would be very important, but that was so far away. These were all things she considered as the semester moved forward.

The guys were getting the top secured on the jeep. "Thanks for helping me with this," Chris said.

"No problem," Austin said. "Those clouds don't look too friendly."

"The week after Easter is supposed to be really nice. We'll get the top back off and make the Lucy Loop a few more times."

"You're not making it easy to be a good boy."

"Hey," Chris said, "there's nothing wrong with looking. And they wouldn't be out sunbathing if they weren't comfortable with it."

"You think?" Austin asked. "Just because they are working on their tan doesn't necessarily mean they want an audience."

"Maybe not all of them. But if they didn't want an audience, why weren't they sunbathing outside the entrance facing Hamilton Hall? There's no road that goes by that side, and this time of day, it's getting just as much sun as the side we drove by. You saw how many threw up their hands and waved as we drove by. I'm telling you: Girls love a guy in a jeep."

Austin considered this. Almost everyone had waved at them. They were checking out the sunbathers, but they were checking them out too. And just as the only thing he knew about the ladies were what they looked like, all they knew about him and Chris were that they were in a jeep. Did that somehow make them look more rugged and manly?

With the cover back on the jeep, the two began walking towards the Tiger's Den. "It's just harmless flirting," Chris said. "There's nothing wrong with looking. Trust me, it's not hurting anyone."

"I suppose," Austin said as they opened the door to go inside.

The four enjoyed lunch, and afterwards, Chris and Austin dropped off Amanda and Hannah at the library. They all finished out the short week of classes and each left campus to visit their respective families over the long weekend.

Easter Sunday came and Austin attended church with his family. The church his family attended when they went was one of the most widely attended of any in his town, and the numbers grew even higher on Christmas and Easter. However, it was not the crowd size that caught Austin's attention. With the warmer weather that had arrived and it being a special Sunday, many ladies were wearing spring dresses. Some had on extremely short skirts. It was the Lucy Loop all over again. After spending all winter with everyone wearing jeans and sweatshirts, Austin found his eyes being drawn to the ladies in attendance.

Austin thought about how much the setting mattered. In the Lucy Loop, he was observing women laying out in bathing suits. Weren't they asking to be noticed? And were they waving at him and Chris just to flirt? Chris seemed to think the fact they were in a jeep didn't hurt their chances for some innocent flirting. This, however, was Easter Sunday, and he was at church. But that didn't change the fact that some of the dresses were quite revealing. He knew that not everyone on campus was a Christian and dressed modestly. Some probably enjoyed the attention. But this was church! Shouldn't these women have some responsibility to help the guys out by not revealing so much? Is their choice of dress giving him permission to look? Regardless of the ladies' responsibilities, Austin knew he needed to at least make an effort to remember what was being celebrated today.

He tried to focus on the service and the sermon about the meaning of Christ's resurrection. Staying focused proved hard, but Austin decided to take notes on the sermon to keep his mind focused on why he was at church in the first place. He knew that keeping his mind focused on the right things would not be any easier when he got back to campus.

Scripture

Matthew 5:27-30

You have heard that it was said, 'You shall not commit adultery.' But I tell you that anyone who looks at a woman lustfully has already committed adultery with her in his heart. If your right eye causes you to stumble, gouge it out and throw it away. It is better for you to lose one part of your body than for your whole body to be thrown into hell. And if your right hand causes you to stumble, cut it off and throw it away. It is better for you to lose one part of your body than for your whole body to go into hell.

1 Corinthians 6:18-20

Flee from sexual immorality. All other sins a person commits are outside the body, but whoever sins sexually, sins against their own body. Do you not know that your bodies are temples of the Holy Spirit, who is in you, whom you have received from God? You are not your own; you were bought at a price. Therefore, honor God with your bodies.

1 John 2:15-17

Do not love the world or anything in the world. If anyone loves the world, love for the Father is not in them. For everything in the world—the lust of the flesh, the lust of the eyes, and the pride of life—comes not from the Father but from the world. The world and its desires pass away, but whoever does the will of God lives forever.

1 Thessalonians 4:3-8

It is God's will that you should be sanctified: that you should avoid sexual immorality; that each of you should learn to control your own body in a way that is holy and honorable, not in passionate lust like the pagans, who do not know God; and that in this matter no one should wrong or take advantage of a brother or sister. The Lord will punish all those who commit such sins, as we told you and warned you before. For God did not call us to be impure, but to live a holy life. Therefore, anyone who rejects this instruction does not reject a human being but God, the very God who gives you his Holy Spirit.

Questions

1. In your small groups, read each of the scripture verses. As you read them, consider:

    a. Matthew 5:27-30. Austin and Hannah both struggle with knowing what is right. If you apply this verse to the story told in this chapter, where would you tell them that the line is between right and wrong?

    b. 1 Corinthians 6:18-20, These verses remind us both that Jesus paid the price for our sins and that the Holy Spirit dwells in every believer. What does it look like to honor God with your body? When we are told to flee from sexual immorality, what does that look like in practice? Does it only apply to the literal act of sexual intercourse? What else could it apply to?

    c. 1 John 2:15-17. What instructions are we given in these verses? What does it mean to you when it says that "whoever does the will of God lives forever"?

    d. 1 Thessalonians 4:3-8. What does it mean to be both holy and honorable in the way you control your body? What are some ways that we take advantage of our brothers and sisters in Christ? When we do wrong other believers, do you consider that we are not just treating them poorly but also are rejecting God?

2. In the story, Chris and Amanda intentionally sought out opportunities to see members of the opposite sex where they could admire their physical appearance. How are their motives and actions different than that of Austin and Hannah?

3. Hannah and Austin found themselves tempted in different situations. Hannah did not realize the group would be driving by the male athlete's residence hall. Austin did not expect to be so drawn to the women at his church. How would you respond if you were in their positions?

4. The responsibilities of men and women to honor the opposite sex can be a controversial topic. When it comes to how we dress, what are the responsibilities of men? What are the responsibilities of women? What does popular culture say about this issue?

5. Chris defends his actions by saying that the women they observe sunbathing like the attention. One side of the building does not have vehicle access, and the residents could easily sunbathe on that side. How would you respond to Chris's rationale? Even if the men playing sports and women out sunbathing do like the attention, what would be the best way for us to honor God in how we choose to think and act?

6. How do you go about setting healthy limits and boundaries when you are dating someone?

7. What can we do to avoid situations where we might face the temptation to dishonor other men and women? While we can choose not to put ourselves in a setting where we are tempted, we may still struggle

with inappropriate thoughts. How can we respond when we are tempted to go places in our mind that we ought not go?

Challenge for the Week

Take time this week to reflect on the lesson. Reread the scripture verses and reflect on the discussion that your group had as you went through the questions. As you reflect, consider what living out the scripture verses would look like in today's world.

CHAPTER 9

Leadership Team

Matt was walking through the library when he saw Lauren sitting at a table looking over some papers. He approached her and said, "Hey, Lauren, I'm surprised to see you here."

Lauren looked puzzled as she responded, "Why is that?"

"Didn't you just have your big British literature test yesterday?"

"Yeah," Lauren said. "And I'm glad that's over with."

"I figured you would be taking a break from the books today."

"Oh, I'm not studying. I'm looking at something for next year."

"What's that?" Matt asked.

"Here, take a look," Lauren said as she motioned for him to sit down.

Matt sat down and looked at the packet Lauren handed him. It was a list of service positions for Campus Christian Assembly, referred to by students as CCA. By each position, there was a short description of the duties required.

"Are you thinking of getting more involved?" Matt asked.

"I am. These are all the service positions that are part of the leadership team."

Matt glanced over some of the pages. "Your schedule is going to be overflowing if you add this onto your classes and the time required by the marching band. Are you sure you want that heavy of a load?"

"I love being in the band, but it takes so much of my time. I want the opportunity to try some different things, so I'm not going to be in the band next year."

"Wow, that's a big decision. So, which one of the service positions are you going to go for?"

"I've just read over the list once, but four of them jumped out at me. The first one is Lunch Bunch. Every Monday, a local church provides lunch for CCA. The Lunch Bunch coordinator makes sure there is a host church each week as well as someone to provide a written devotion for people to read."

"That sounds manageable," Matt said. "Seems like it would be busy on the front end, but once you got everything lined up for the semester, it wouldn't be too demanding of your time."

"I think it would just take good coordination to make sure each week is covered. If I did this one, I would also line up volunteers to reach out to anyone new or that they see eating alone."

"What else are you considering?"

Lauren went on to describe the three other positions. The Fellowship Coordinator would be responsible for planning the various CCA activities and events throughout the school year. This person would also work to promote them and make sure people felt welcome at the events. The Worship Leader was in charge of the weekly worship time each Tuesday night. Duties would involve making sure someone was prepared to lead in a time of music to be followed by a devotion. Any announcements for upcoming events would also be included. Lastly, there was the Small Groups Coordinator. This position lined up leaders for small group Bible studies that would meet throughout the semester. The person in this role would work to support these group leaders by helping find materials for the weekly lessons and talking through any issues or concerns the small group leaders had.

"They all sound like good ways to get involved. Is there one that stands out to you?" Matt asked.

"Not yet, but I literally just read over the descriptions of each position. I'm not sure which one would be the best fit."

"How are people selected for these positions?" Matt asked. "What happens when more than one person expresses interest?"

"Anyone interested in serving puts down their top three choices and writes a summary of why they believe they would succeed in the role. Then the campus minister and a few others from a local church that partners with CCA decide who will serve in each area. The president is the only exception, and it is decided by student vote."

"I see, so you aren't guaranteed to get the position you decide you would like the most."

"That's right," Lauren said, nodding her head.

"I love being around people," Matt added. "That fellowship position sounds like it would be a lot of fun."

"It would, but it would be a lot of work too. You have to find out what people enjoy doing and how costly those things would be. CCA could help with some of the cost but not all. And we are just poor college students."

"That's true," Matt acknowledged. "But there are a lot of budget-friendly options. We get into football and basketball games free. Other campus events are usually cheap if not totally free. There are lots of trails nearby that don't cost anything to hike. And your standard bowling night wouldn't cost that much."

"It would be fun. Granted, there would be a time commitment in planning and promoting those events."

"What do you think your gifts are?" Matt asked. "What do you enjoy doing?"

"I do enjoy getting to know people, but I'm nowhere near the extrovert you are. I feel like I'm a creative person. That's why I joined the marching band. I'm organized. I have to be to keep up with my classwork and the time that the band requires. And I try to maintain some sort of social life on top of all that."

"We've had some deep conversations too. I feel like you are a wise person. A few times when I was dealing with different issues, you gave me great advice."

Lauren smiled. "Thank you. That's very kind."

"What about the other two? Worship and small groups?"

"Worship would be a big responsibility. Your Tuesday nights are shot. There is a praise band that plays most weeks, but you still have to make sure someone is scheduled each week. And you want people to lead meaningful devotions. But you can't schedule speakers too far in advance, because you need to be aware of the needs of the students throughout the semester."

"That's a lot to be responsible for."

"I wouldn't be on my own. The campus minister helps too. But there is also a practical matter."

"What's that?" Matt asked.

"There is a humanities class I really want to take. But there aren't many times it is offered. A lot of them are on Tuesday afternoons and early evening."

"Even if you waited until next spring, there's no guarantee they would be offered at more convenient times."

"Exactly," Lauren said. "And I really want to finish up the general core by the end of next year.

"There is still the Small Groups Coordinator. What about it?"

"That one looks really good. I would enjoy getting to know the people leading the smaller Bible studies and supporting them. Even if I end up with a Tuesday night class, I could schedule different times throughout the week to meet with them and look at the needs of their groups."

Matt handed the list of service positions back to Lauren. "Well," he said, "I think you would be good at any of these, but I agree that you are organized, and I think you are wise. Lunch Bunch and Small Groups are the two I think you'd be best at."

"I do think I'd be better suited to those. Now it's just a matter of deciding which one to list as my top choice."

"Good luck. I'll be curious to hear what you decide."

Scripture

1 Corinthians 12:4-26

There are different kinds of gifts, but the same Spirit distributes them. There are different kinds of service, but the same Lord. There are different kinds of working, but in all of them and in everyone it is the same God at work.

Now to each one the manifestation of the Spirit is given for the common good. To one there is given through the Spirit a message of wisdom, to another a message of knowledge by means of the same Spirit, to another faith by the same Spirit, to another gifts of healing by that one Spirit, to another miraculous powers, to another prophecy, to another distinguishing between spirits, to another speaking in different kinds of tongues, and to still another the interpretation of tongues. All these are the work of one and the same Spirit, and he distributes them to each one, just as he determines.

Just as a body, though one, has many parts, but all its many parts form one body, so it is with Christ. For we were all baptized by one Spirit so as to form one body—whether Jews or Gentiles, slave or free—and we were all given the one Spirit to drink. Even so the body is not made up of one part but of many.

Now if the foot should say, "Because I am not a hand, I do not belong to the body," it would not for that reason stop being part of the body. And if the ear should say, "Because I am not an eye, I do not belong to the body," it would not for that reason stop being part of the body. If the whole body were an eye, where would the sense of hearing be? If the whole body were an ear, where would the sense of smell be? But in fact God has placed the parts in the body, every one of them, just as he wanted them to be. If they were all one part, where would the body be? As it is, there are many parts, but one body.

The eye cannot say to the hand, "I don't need you!" And the head cannot say to the feet, "I don't need you!" On the contrary, those parts of the body that seem to be weaker are indispensable, and the parts that we think are less honorable we treat with special honor. And the parts that are unpresentable are treated with special modesty, while our presentable parts need no special treatment. But God has put the body together, giving greater honor to the parts that lacked it, so that there should be no division in the body, but that its parts should have equal concern for each other. If one part suffers, every part suffers with it; if one part is honored, every part rejoices with it.

Romans 12:3-8

For by the grace given me I say to every one of you: Do not think of yourself more highly than you ought, but rather think of yourself with sober judgment, in accordance with the faith God has distributed to each of you. For just as each of us has one body with many members, and these members do not all have the same function, so in Christ we, though many, form one body, and each member belongs to all the others. We have different gifts, according to the grace given to each of us. If your gift is prophesying, then prophesy in accordance with your faith; if it is serving, then serve; if it is teaching, then teach; if it is to encourage, then give encouragement; if it is giving, then give generously; if it is to lead, do it diligently; if it is to show mercy, do it cheerfully.

Questions

1. According to the scripture from 1 Corinthians, who distributes spiritual gifts to believers? What are some of the gifts mentioned in both scripture passages for this chapter?

2. Every believer has at least one gift. The passage from Romans tells us to use our gifts cheerfully. What are some of your strengths? What brings you joy? Based on your answers to those questions, what gift or gifts do you feel you have? Where do you see opportunities in your life to use your gifts?

3. We may feel tempted to compare our gifts to the gifts we see in others. How can the scripture from 1 Corinthians help when we are tempted to believe that the gifts we see in others are better or more important than ours? How can the scripture from Romans help when we are tempted to believe our gifts are better or more important than the gifts we see in others?

4. Lauren is trying to decide the best place for her to serve. Of the four options, which is most appealing to you? Which is least? What does that tell you about your own interests and what your strengths might be?

Challenge for the Week

Reflect this week on the discussion of spiritual gifts. Compare the gifts you see in yourself, the gifts others see in you, and the results of any spiritual gifts inventory completed in your group. Pray that God would help you see opportunities to use these gifts and for courage in cases where you may feel hesitant about putting your gifts into action.

CHAPTER 10

The Catalyst

Amanda arrived at the CCA House and sat down on one of the couches. The CCA House was the student center for the Campus Christian Assembly. She had arrived early to meet a few friends there to go get lunch. She laid her head back and shut her eyes, feeling mentally exhausted from the probability and statistics test she had just finished.

While she was resting, Steve and Michelle came in. Steve was the campus minister, and Michelle was a staff member at a local church that partnered with CCA. They noticed Amanda sitting on the couch.

"Rough day?" Michelle asked.

Amanda opened her eyes and replied, "Tough test. I almost didn't finish the last problem before time ran out."

"Well, at least it's over now," Steve said. "What are you doing with the rest of your day?"

"Meeting some friends for lunch, but their science lab doesn't let out for another half hour," Amanda answered.

Steve and Michelle looked at each other. Michelle nodded and spoke. "Amanda, could we talk to you in the office before your friends get here?"

Amanda wondered what they might want. "Sure, we can talk."

She followed them up to the office. Steve unlocked the door, and then he, Michelle, and Amanda all went in and sat down. Steve offered Amanda a water from the mini-fridge beside his desk, which she declined.

Steve began the conversation. "Amanda, what are you plans for the summer?"

"I haven't really settled on anything yet," she answered. "I'm not taking any summer classes. I'll probably visit my grandparents at some point. Other than that, I'll probably just be working."

"We'd like you to consider an opportunity we know of this summer," Steve continued. "Have you heard of Community Connectors?"

Amanda shook her head. "No, I'm not familiar with it."

"Community Connectors is a local outreach organization that matches church groups looking for service projects with families that are in need of home repairs. I'm friends with the program administrator. He reached out to me asking if I knew any students that might be potential summer staff for the program. Michelle and I were talking and we both thought you would be a good fit."

"I hope you don't mind, but I told Steve about the conversation we had in our small group at church a few weeks ago," Michelle said. "During a lesson from the book of Ezra, we were talking about being catalysts for God. When we see a need and have an opportunity to help, we can honor God by doing so. You mentioned feeling like this was an area of life where you would like to grow."

"I remember," Amanda said. "I just didn't know where to start. The application deadlines have passed for so many summer outreach programs. Plus, if I get a job back home, I don't know what my schedule would be."

Michelle continued, "Community Connectors still has a few staff spots available. It is a paid position, so you would be able to build some savings as summer staff."

"What's involved?" Amanda asked. "What does summer staff do?"

Steve answered, "A staff person is assigned to each church group that comes in. The groups will be made up of some adults but mainly high school students. You work with a group each week at the site of a home being repaired. The church groups will have people with the carpentry skills to make sure the work gets done. Your role will be to get to know the groups coming in and be an encouragement to them. You'll also be helping with the home repairs, but again, the groups will have people with them that have the carpentry skills to do any sawing or cutting."

"You'll also get to know the people who live in the homes you are working on," Michelle said. "It's a way to show God's love through the service, but you can also build relationships with the homeowners and the different groups that do the repairs. Staff members also lead a worship service at the beginning and end of each week with the groups coming in."

Amanda looked puzzled. "Why are you asking me? I'm not sure I'd be very good at it."

Michelle smiled. "I've observed how good you are at making new people feel welcome here. So, I already know you are a great encourager and great at making people feel at ease in a new environment. As far as the home repairs go, it isn't that hard to learn to paint and to put down shingles on a roof. A lot of the students you meet will be learning those skills too. After the first week or two, you'll be a pro whereas each new group you meet will have students just learning those skills."

"Thank you for saying that. It does sound like a good opportunity," Amanda said. "I remember our conversation during the study of Ezra. It's hard to put into words, but during our conversation I just felt like I should be using this time in my life to serve and grow in my faith. And I don't know how many chances I'll have to commit the kind of time a project like Community Connectors would require. I'd like to think about it. How long would I have to let you know?"

Steve said, "There are still two staff positions available. The director is trying to fill them as soon as possible. I can set up an interview if you'd like to speak with him. He would be able to tell you more specifics about the program."

"Sure, I'd like that," Amanda said.

"Ok, I'll see if he is free to come by Tuesday before our service," Steve said.

Amanda heard voices downstairs and said, "Science lab must have finished early. I'm going to head out. Thanks for talking with me about this. I appreciate your thinking of me."

Steve and Michelle both smiled and they said their goodbyes.

After Amanda left, Steve looked at Michelle and asked, "Well, what do you think?"

"I think she'd be great at it. And I can tell she was interested. She just needs some encouragement to know she would be great at it. She is fantastic when it comes to making guests at church feel comfortable, and she has been a hard worker on any service project we've ever done together."

"We've opened the door. I'll get the interview set up as soon as I can. Then we'll just wait and see what happens."

Scripture

Ezra 1:1-4

In the first year of Cyrus king of Persia, in order to fulfill the word of the LORD spoken by Jeremiah, the LORD moved the heart of Cyrus king of Persia to make a proclamation throughout his realm and also to put it in writing:

"This is what Cyrus king of Persia says:

> 'The LORD, the God of heaven, has given me all the kingdoms of the earth and he has appointed me to build a temple for him at Jerusalem in Judah. Any of his people among you may go up to Jerusalem in Judah and build the temple of the LORD, the God of Israel, the God who is in Jerusalem, and may their God be with them. And in any locality where survivors may now be living, the people are to provide them with silver and gold, with goods and livestock, and with freewill offerings for the temple of God in Jerusalem.'"

Ezra 7:8-10

Ezra arrived in Jerusalem in the fifth month of the seventh year of the king. He had begun his journey from Babylon on the first day of the first month, and he arrived in Jerusalem on the first day of the fifth month, for the gracious hand of his God was on him. For Ezra had devoted himself to the study and observance of the Law of the LORD, and to teaching its decrees and laws in Israel.

Ezra 9:1-4

After these things had been done, the leaders came to me and said, "The people of Israel, including the priests and the Levites, have not kept themselves separate from the neighboring peoples with their detestable practices, like those of the Canaanites, Hittites, Perizzites, Jebusites, Ammonites, Moabites, Egyptians and Amorites. They have taken some of their daughters as wives for themselves and their sons, and have mingled the holy race with the peoples around them. And the leaders and officials have led the way in this unfaithfulness."

When I heard this, I tore my tunic and cloak, pulled hair from my head and beard and sat down appalled. Then everyone who trembled at the words of the God of Israel gathered around me because of this unfaithfulness of the exiles. And I sat there appalled until the evening sacrifice.

Ezra 10:1-4

While Ezra was praying and confessing, weeping and throwing himself down before the house of God, a large crowd of Israelites—men, women and children—gathered around him. They too wept bitterly. Then Shekaniah son of Jehiel, one of the descendants of Elam, said to Ezra, "We have been unfaithful to our God by marrying foreign women from the peoples around us. But in spite of this, there is still hope for Israel. Now let us make a covenant before our God to send away all these women and their children, in accordance with the counsel of my lord and of those who fear the commands of our God. Let it be done according to the Law. Rise up; this matter is in your hands. We will support you, so take courage and do it."

Questions

1. Answer the following questions relating to the scripture reading from Ezra:

    a. 1:1-4, Cyrus, king of Persia, was not a follower of God. How is God active even in the king's life, despite him not worshipping God? What encouragement can this give when we feel like God is not active in our lives or the world around us?

    b. 7:8-10. Ezra devoted himself to studying, practicing, and teaching the Law. While we are no longer under the Law, studying scripture, putting God's love into practice through our actions, and sharing our faith are all still important. Which of these do you feel you are best at? Which of these is most difficult for you? Why?

    c. 9:1-4. What are the people of Israel doing that upsets Ezra?

    d. 10:1-4. Ezra is a catalyst for the people of Israel returning to God. Through his actions, the people of Israel are inspired to repent and turn from their sin. Even catalysts can need encouragement. How do the people of Israel encourage Ezra?

2. In the story, how are Steve and Michelle catalysts for Amanda?

3. If Amanda chooses to apply for the summer staff position, how could she be a catalyst for the people she would meet over the summer?

4. A catalyst sees a need and takes responsibility for it. Ezra found the people of Israel engaged in sin and took action to address it. However, not everything in life is our responsibility. How would you seek wisdom and discernment to know when it is appropriate for you to address a problem?

Challenge for the Week

In this study, many ways to be a catalyst for God are discussed. Watch for opportunities to be a catalyst this week. This could be praying for someone or encouraging them. It could mean directly getting involved somewhere that you see an unmet need. Pray for wisdom that God would reveal the best course of action to take.

CHAPTER 11

Dead Week Decisions

Campus looked like a ghost town from the outside. But one only had to look inside the library to find the missing student body. The week before finals was called Dead Week. Usually during this time there would not be tests or new projects assigned. Normal instruction would continue and any projects not already finished would be due. Many students had waited until the last minute to finish up these projects. Those finishing up research and group projects could be found in the library or at home typing out their papers.

Brandon sat deep in thought at a table in the library. His thoughts, however, were not about the research paper due at the end of the week. When the semester was over, he needed to decide how he would spend his summer. To anyone walking by, it looked like Brandon was staring off into space, but really he was lost in his head considering each option.

I should definitely take the landscaping job, he thought. Instead of being stuck inside, I'd be out mowing yards and doing landscaping for different customers. I hate getting up so early, but I'd have my evenings free and be off every weekend. I'd have so much time to hang out with my friends, and I'd be able to get back into church and see my friends. Well, I guess I'd have time to do stuff with my friends. If work starts at 7 a.m., what time would I have to go to bed? But there would still be Friday night and Saturday.

Landscaping would be the right choice financially too. It's a 40-hour-per-week job. It pays better that a lot of part-time jobs. My parents have been so generous in helping with my tuition. It really limited the amount of student loans I needed this year. I need to make my own contribution in a big way.

But what about the beach trip? So many of my friends are going to be on that trip in July, and I already know I can't take any time off from that job in July. Still, there will be plenty of other things to do with my friends over the summer. And the point of the job is to make money for school. A week at the beach would certainly eat into my savings. Yes, that's the right choice. I'll take the job and enjoy seeing friends on nights and weekends. I'll bet there will be some weekend trips I can be part of. But how many spur-of-the-moment trips would I miss? Ugh! I just don't know.

The next option was to get a part-time job at a restaurant or possibly work at a store in the mall. That's what I need to do, Brandon thought. My schedule would be so much more flexible. I'd be working with other high school and college kids. I'd still be making money, even if it wasn't as much as landscaping and mowing. It would be a lot easier to switch schedules and get time off. I'd definitely be able to go on the beach trip then. And honestly, the work would be easier. I'm sure there would be plenty to do in any job, but I'd have more time to get to know my coworkers than if I'm out mowing all day. Depending on where I got a job, I might even be able to work with some of my friends. That would be fantastic! How great would it be to get paid for hanging out with his friends? I could stay out later on my nights off since I wouldn't have to be up so early each day.

Then he thought about his family again, and he thought about how much help they gave him. The money they provided to help with my tuition was huge, he thought. I would earn quite a bit less if I just work a retail or restaurant job. And if I go to the beach, that's going to eat up a lot of what I do put back in savings. I can't do that to my family.

I really want to reconnect with my friends, though. When we got together over Christmas, I could already see how some of us had started to drift apart. It's only going to get worse, he thought, as some older kids from church came to mind. Friends that graduated high school ahead of him had come home the first two summers they were in college. But he had found out that some were staying in their college town to either take summer classes or internships related to their majors. Brandon thought about the limited time he had. I may only have two or three summers left. I want to keep these connections as long as I can. Of course, I've made some really great friends this past year too. With the flexibility of a part-time job, I could travel back to campus a few times over the summer and visit with my college friends that live close to campus. I just don't know.

A third option would be to spend the summer working at a camp near his hometown. Mountain View Outreach was a Christian camp that hosted a different group of campers each week. Maybe I need to accept the offer to serve as a camp counselor. I loved going there when I was younger. I already know a lot of the returning staff, and there were fun new people to meet every year I went. I wouldn't have any transportation or meal costs.

Brandon grimaced, however, as he thought about the negatives. I'd miss the beach trip. Of course, that was going to be a big expense anyway. He had just thought about the limited time he may have left with his high school friends. Working at the camp would take even more time away than if he took the landscaping job. The thought of the landscaping job brought his mind back to the financial side of the equation. Serving at the camp would pay even less than working a part-time job. Even without transportation or meal expenses, he would still be worse off financially than with either of the other two options.

Then he thought about the purpose of the camp. It was a lot of fun, and there were great people to meet, but the purpose was to grow in your faith. As a counselor, he could do for campers what the counselors had done for him when he attended. That would be to share his faith, to serve, and to invest in the lives of others. That was something he could not put a price tag on. And how many times in his life could he do something like this?

Once I'm of college, I'll have a full-time job and one day, hopefully, a family. The opportunity to do something like this for an entire summer just won't be there. I would not make as much money, and I'd miss out on a summer with so many old friends. But isn't that what living out my faith looks like—service and sacrifice? The thought of post-college responsibilities brought his mind back to a part-time job. The opportunities to have a fun summer hanging out with my friends are also limited. I need to spend time over the summer with them while I still can.

Something else occurred to him about his faith. The summer camp will not be my only option to share my faith with people. I would get to know people at any job. And whether landscaping or working part-time, I'll still see all my old friends. I could invest in those relationships and look for chances to serve and live out my faith. He thought of Jacob, a friend he had last seen over Christmas break. Jacob had really drifted from the church and pretty much admitted to not being a Christian. Brandon knew that Jacob was going to be home for the summer. His would definitely be a life worth investing in, Brandon thought.

Brandon bounced back and forth between his three options, unable to make a decision. How should he prioritize all the options he was weighing? He needed to honor his parents and contribute to the cost of his education. The landscaping job definitely checked that box, but he could still save some money working somewhere part-time. He needed to be aware that this time in his life would not last forever. He thought about how he could honor the friendships he had, and honestly, he wanted to enjoy the opportunity for a summer that was a little more carefree. His college years were a special time in his life, and they would not last forever. He would have the rest of his life to work. And besides a planned trip to the beach, who knew what other spontaneous trips might happen? Would serving at camp be the best way to honor God? His church talked a lot about trusting God. So, if camp didn't offer a lot financially, should he trust God to provide the cost of tuition? And did trust God really mean taking out bigger student loans and trusting his parents to cover the rest?

Brandon was getting nowhere. He was thinking in circles. There was still time to weigh his options, but he would need to decide by the end of the semester, which was less than two weeks away. He did know one thing for sure. If he didn't get back to his schoolwork, he would be repeating several of his classes next semester. Brandon sighed and started reviewing his research notes.

Scripture

James 1:5

If any of you lacks wisdom, you should ask God, who gives generously to all without finding fault, and it will be given to you.

Proverbs 12:15

The way of fools seems right to them,
but the wise listen to advice.

Philippians 4:6-7

Do not be anxious about anything, but in every situation, by prayer and petition, with thanksgiving, present your requests to God. And the peace of God, which transcends all understanding, will guard your hearts and your minds in Christ Jesus.

Genesis 2:19-20

Now the Lord God had formed out of the ground all the wild animals and all the birds in the sky. He brought them to the man to see what he would name them; and whatever the man called each living creature, that was its name. So, the man gave names to all the livestock, the birds in the sky and all the wild animals.

Questions

1. Think of a time you had to make an important decision. How did you weigh each option in order to make your decision?

2. In the story, Brandon is facing three choices. What are the pros and cons of each option? (You might think of some that were not specifically mentioned in the reading.)

3. Read the scripture verses one at a time. As you read each one, consider:

    a. James 1:5. Who is someone in your life that you consider to be a wise person? What is it about them that makes you consider them to be wise? In what ways do you think God provides wisdom?

    b. Proverbs 12:15. This verse says that the wise listen to advice. However, not everyone is wise or has your best interests at heart. When you need advice, how do you choose to whom you will listen?

    c. Philippians 4:6-7. There are many things in life that can cause anxiety. We may face difficult relationships, challenging classes, and health concerns both for ourselves and our family members. Given these life circumstances, how would you put these verses in practice?

d. Genesis 2:19-20. In these verses, we see that after God created all the animals, it was man that named them. This teaches us that God created us to be decision makers. Have you ever considered that God has given us the responsibility to make wise choices concerning our lives? How do you process your options when facing a difficult decision? Is it possible that sometimes there isn't a "right" or "wrong" answer and that you can honor God as long as you do your best at whatever you choose? Once you have made a decision, what are some ways you can honor God as you implement that decision?

4. How could you honor God in any of the summer options that were presented? If you were in Brandon's position, what decision would you make? How did you arrive at your decision?

Challenge for the Week

This lesson is about using wisdom to make decisions. Take time this week to memorize the scripture verses for this chapter. Pray that God would help you to grow in wisdom.

CHAPTER 12

Going Home, Leaving Home

Brandon and Austin's room was in an odd state of transition. If an outsider looked at the room, it would be difficult to tell if they were moving in or moving out. Both of them had finished their final exams but still had two days before they had to be out of the residence hall. They had decided to stick around and attend a party on Thursday to celebrate the end of the school year. In order to be ready to leave on Friday morning, they had already packed up most of their belongings. That left their room looking much more barren than either was used to.

Austin was continuing to pack up while Brandon was at the bookstore selling back some of his textbooks. As he packed, he thought about home. However, he did not think of the home he would be returning to Friday morning. He was thinking of the room where he currently stood. When the school year started, he would use phrases like "I'll meet you back at Cordell" referring to the name of the residence hall or "I'm headed back to the hall after class." At some point, Austin had started calling his room "home." When did this place become home?

Brandon entered the room and dropped his backpack on the couch. "That took longer than I expected. The line at the bookstore was crazy long."

"I need to sell my books back too but keep putting it off," Austin replied. He looked around the room. "It looks kind of depressing, doesn't it?"

"Yeah," Brandon answered. "The sad thing is how much we still have left to pack. I can't believe how much we accumulated over the year."

The walls were bare without any posters or pictures. With most of their clothes already packed, the closet appeared strange having just a few items left on hangers. The residence hall in general was quieter as some students had already left for the summer.

"What are you most looking forward to when you get back to your family's house?" Austin asked.

Brandon answered without a moment's hesitation. "My mom's cooking! I've learned to cook a little this year, but none of it compares to what she makes. How about you?"

"Same thing. The food in the cafeteria is good, but it doesn't compare to what Mom makes. I'm also looking forward to sleeping in my own bed again."

"The mattresses are lumpy, aren't they? Even with my memory foam, it just isn't the same as my bed back home."

As the guys resumed packing, Austin thought about other things he was looking forward to. As much as his little sister could get on his nerves, he was even excited to see her again. Seeing his friends from high school would be great too. Austin was really interested in hearing everyone else's stories from their freshman year. He wondered what changes he might see in them. Then Austin paused as he wondered what changes they might see in him. The past year had been the most challenging of his life. He had entered a new school with a roommate he didn't know. He lived away from home for the first time in his life. He had learned how to live with a roommate as well as neighbors on both sides of his walls. He had taken on the responsibility of attending all his classes, completing his assignments, and studying for tests. There were so many new experiences that Austin could not count them all.

"It will be weird in some ways being back home, though," Austin said.

"How so?" Brandon asked.

"I don't know if my parents are going to try and give me a curfew. I'm used to just going wherever I want whenever I want."

"I hadn't thought of that. I haven't had that conversation with my family either."

"It will also be weird not having people to talk to any time I feel like hanging out."

Brandon's eyes widened. "I hadn't thought of that either. There is always someone to hang out with here. And it's great late at night that you don't even have to go out to find someone to talk to."

"It's going to be great in a lot of ways, but it is also going to be different. I just hope my family recognizes that I've grown, and I don't just mean physically." Austin laughed as he patted his belly. He had heard people talk about the freshman

15, referring to the weight many college students gain during their first year. Austin thought it had certainly applied in his case.

Brandon also laughed. "I agree. I feel more responsible, and I don't just mean with school. I feel like I've grown spiritually too."

Austin also thought about his spiritual growth since starting college. "With so many new things year, I've definitely learned to trust God more, you know? I handle the things I can control and trust God with the rest."

Austin could not control the amount of work his professors gave, but he could manage his time so he didn't become overwhelmed at the end of the semester. He had made wise choices in the friends he made. He had met people of different faiths and people not associated with any organized religion in his classes and among his neighbors in Cordell Hall. And while he wanted to represent his faith to them all, he had learned not to put himself in situations where he would likely make poor choices. When those times came that he did not make wise decisions, Austin had learned gratitude as he experienced God's grace and forgiveness.

"You must have been paying attention in church," Brandon said.

"A little bit," Austin said jokingly. "The recent series has been really good."

"I always wondered why the Bible was full of so many old stories. They are interesting and all, but I didn't really know what I was supposed to get from them until now."

The church Brandon and Austin attended had just finished a series on characters from the Old Testament. Each week, the pastor shared about the life of a different person and how we could gain wisdom today from the situations they faced and the choices they made.

"It was a shocker that there was so much we could get out of things that happened thousands of years ago," Austin said.

"They were definitely different times," Brandon said. "Just think, was there much to do besides farming and fishing back then?"

"They don't have anything like what we do today. The internet, professional sports, amusement parks, funny videos posted online. But a lot of their problems are similar to the same stuff we deal with."

"I liked how the preacher phrased it, 'It's the same dance, just a different tune,'" Brandon said, referring to a recent sermon where the pastor pointed out that a lot of the struggles people have are the same, even though we may live in a time of different customs and advanced technology. People throughout time have dealt with overcoming their pride, jealousy, greed, and problems in their relationships.

Austin thought about that. Despite the challenges of the previous year and the excitement about returning home, Austin realized he was already thinking about the next school year. His sophomore year would be a different tune and bring new challenges of its own, but it would not be nearly as stressful on the front end. He and Brandon were going to be back in the same room, so it wouldn't take anywhere near as long to get things set up as it did this year. They already had what they needed and planned on setting up the room the same as it had been this year. Having Chris and Matt back as their neighbors would be an added bonus. In fact, a lot of the friends they had made in the residence hall were going to be back. He had a good class schedule and had even enrolled in some classes with his friends.

Austin thought about the strong friendships he had made. Perhaps it was the struggles of adjusting to college life that helped form such strong bonds. In a way, Austin had gained another family. As much as he looked forward to getting back to his hometown, he realized how much he would miss this new family he had made.

Thankfully, he didn't have to say goodbye just yet. His exams were over, but he wasn't leaving campus until Friday morning. For the time being, his schedule was wide open. Austin looked out his window and enjoyed the view of campus. As he realized what a great year this had been, Austin found himself filled with a tremendous sense of gratitude.

Brandon checked at the time and said "Hey, we need to get going if we're going to meet Chris and Matt for lunch. Are you ready?"

Austin answered as he reached for his keys and wallet. "You bet!"

Scripture

Matthew 6:25-34

"Therefore, I tell you, do not worry about your life, what you will eat or drink; or about your body, what you will wear. Is not life more than food, and the body more than clothes? Look at the birds of the air; they do not sow or reap or store away in barns, and yet your heavenly Father feeds them. Are you not much more valuable than they? Can any one of you by worrying add a single hour to your life?

"And why do you worry about clothes? See how the flowers of the field grow. They do not labor or spin. Yet I tell you that not even Solomon in all his splendor was dressed like one of these. If that is how God clothes the grass of the field, which is here today and tomorrow is thrown into the fire, will he not much more clothe you—you of little faith? So do not worry, saying, 'What shall we eat?' or 'What shall we drink?' or 'What shall we wear?' For the pagans run after all these things, and your heavenly Father knows that you need them. But seek first his kingdom and his righteousness, and all these things will be given to you as well. Therefore, do not worry about tomorrow, for tomorrow will worry about itself. Each day has enough trouble of its own.

John 16:33

"I have told you these things, so that in me you may have peace. In this world you will have trouble. But take heart! I have overcome the world."

Romans 8:28

And we know that in all things God works for the good of those who love him, who have been called according to his purpose.

Questions

1. In the first chapter, you considered some of the concerns you had about this new phase of life. Look back over your answers to those questions. How do you feel about these challenges now?

2. The scripture from Matthew was also referenced in the first chapter. What were some things you worried about over the course of the school year? How did these issues work out? There are going to be problems to resolve throughout life, but in the problems you faced this past year, did worrying help resolve these issues?

3. In the scripture from John, Jesus tells the difficult truth that we will have problems in life. What encouragement can we take from the way the verse ends?

4. How can the scripture from Romans be applied to your life, knowing that life will not always be perfect?

5. What are the different kinds of family a person can have? Who do you consider to be your family?

6. What is your definition of home? Austin feels like he has two homes now. Where do you consider to be home? Do you think it is possible for a person to have more than one home?

7. What are your concerns about the summer? It is important to have people in our lives that we can count on for help and to give us wise advice. Who will be your support system over the summer?

8. If you could send a letter to yourself the first week of classes, what advice would you give yourself?

Challenge for the Week

The last question asked what you would tell yourself the first week of classes. Take time to write a letter to your earlier self. Save it and read it at the beginning of the next school year. Use the advice for your earlier self to help the incoming freshmen you meet during the next school year.

Bonus Challenge

Set a realistic goal to memorize the scripture from this study. In the weeks and months ahead, pray that God would bring these verses to mind when you are in situations where you would benefit from the wisdom contained in these verses.

Notes for Discussion Leaders

First, I would like to thank you for taking on the role of leading and facilitating the conversations that will rise out of this study. As you prepare for each week's study, I would encourage you to consider a good icebreaker to open with before you get into the contents of the chapter. It should be a lighthearted question that everyone will feel comfortable answering. A good icebreaker will also set group members at ease and make them more comfortable sharing when you get to the more serious discussion questions.

Another suggestion for both leaders and group members is to preview the scripture that goes with each lesson. But I would encourage going one step further. To get an accurate context of the scripture referenced in each lesson, take time to read the entire chapter of the Bible in which the verses are found.

Each chapter has questions to help guide the discussion. As the facilitator, you may want to add some of your own questions to help keep the conversation going. This leader's guide will point out places where group members may feel awkward or there may be disagreement. Part of your role will be to preview chapters and consider how you can help discussions to remain respectful.

As you structure each week's lesson, a suggested template for each lesson is provided. However, you should feel free to set up each study according to the needs of your group. You can also add items to or remove items from this outline according to the time constraints of your group:

- Welcome/announcements
- Opening prayer
- Icebreaker question
- Read aloud the story and scripture
- Discussion questions
- Challenge for the Week
- Prayer requests
- Closing prayer

This study has value for any college student, but it will be especially significant in the lives of freshmen. The first year of college can be both exciting and scary. I hope this study helps students at any level to know they are not alone in this experience. You as facilitator can be a great source of strength and encouragement to the students in your group. Some of these chapters present the characters with choices. Help your group members to realize there is not always a right or wrong answer. The emphasis should be on honoring God in whatever choice is made.

Chapter 1 – Orientation

This chapter starts at the moment Brandon's family leaves him to get settled into his residence hall. As you lead the discussion around this chapter, think back to your own experiences at the beginning of your freshman year. You might also draw on experiences when you were in a new setting.

As you prepare for this week's lesson, consider:

- What were your fears and concerns? How did you handle them?
- How did you go about meeting people?
- How did you decide which campus organizations to join?
- How did you handle some of the practical issues, such as finding your classes, learning to live in a smaller space than you may be used to, and learning to live with others, either as a roommate or just in a residence hall full of other people?

The scripture verses point out that God remains the same and is worthy of our trust. Discuss what that looks like in action. What do we do in those moments we feel anxious?

One decision Brandon faces is which student groups he will join. Group members may not agree on their answers, and that is not a bad thing. Some may feel joining a faith-based organization is the "right" answer for a Bible study. Help them to see that you can honor God in any of the groups. Some may choose to join more than one group. Discuss ways to make sure you do not overcommit and sacrifice your academic performance. Again, there is not a right or wrong answer, but help your group to weigh the pros and cons of each decision.

One point to make is in the opportunity to let people know why you are serving. Great service can come from a college or neighborhood group. However, when you serve through a church or campus ministry, those you are serving know that your faith is the motivating factor in your service. With secular organizations, they would not know what reasons the volunteers are there for. It could be faith related, but could also be out a desire to make the neighborhood better or to meet a requirement for school or work. Serving with a faith-based organization provides a ministry opportunity just by people seeing the service occurring.

A counterpoint to this would be in sharing your faith with other volunteers. In a secular service group, people will be volunteering for a variety of reasons. The opportunity might arise to let them know that you are serving because of your faith. And you can always watch for opportunities to share with the people being served.

Again, the point here is not to pick a "right" or "wrong" choice but just to see the opportunities that each choice brings.

A good icebreaker question for this lesson might be to ask members to name something that surprised them when they started college.

Chapter 2 – Sunday Lunch

This chapter is mainly about Austin's experiences as an employee at a restaurant, but it opens with a side story about playing capture the flag. Sometimes Christians can be stereotyped as not being able to have fun. In this lesson, be prepared to help your group discuss ways you can combat this stereotype.

In the story, Austin felt pressure to represent Christ in a positive way. Group members may feel pressured that they will let God down if they do not always represent Christ well. Help them understand we will all fail at times. Remind them of God's grace and that nothing we do can cause God to love us any more or any less.

The customers that are the most difficult to serve are those that have just come from church. Obviously, not all of them are going to be difficult, but there are enough in this story to give the church a bad name. Help your group discuss ways to turn around the negative image of Christians that some people hold. When we feel insignificant or that our small acts of kindness don't make a difference, consider reasons that our actions do matter.

Part of the discussion will involve determining the difference between treatment you may not like and abusive behavior. You might use an example to illustrate this point. If you feel some employees always get better shifts than you, you may view that as unfair. However, if your supervisor is verbally or physically abusive toward employees, that is a much more serious offense. Use this as an opportunity to discuss appropriate boundaries. An expression group members may know is that people should "turn the other cheek" when wronged and show forgiveness. Discuss when that may not be the best response, such as when actual abuse is occurring. When you discuss the scripture, make sure group members know that submitting to those in authority does not mean allowing yourself to be abused.

Chapter 3 – Student Workers

In this chapter, Hannah has to decide whether to tell Amanda about an on-campus job opening. The scripture verses will help generate discussion about what decision Hannah should make. Some group members may struggle with the meaning of the passage from Galatians. In the discussion questions for this chapter, our burdens are compared to different size rocks. Help them to understand that in verse two, we are to carry each other's burdens when we face overwhelming life circumstances such as a death in the family or a job loss. These would be the large boulders of life. In verse five, where we are told to carry our own load, it is referring to our daily responsibilities. These small rocks would include routine responsibilities such as doing laundry, studying, and doing our homework. Your discussion may also involve medium boulders. These would be important decisions such as choosing a major. These are ultimately our responsibility, but we may seek out advice from trusted friends before making these decisions.

Group members may disagree on what Hannah should do. Scripture says to treat others the way we want to be treated. Scripture also says we are to take care of our own daily responsibilities. Watching for an on-campus job is ultimately Amanda's responsibility. However, it would show kindness on Hannah's part to tell her about the position. Group members will need to work through the process of deciding what they would do if in Hannah's position. If your group members do disagree, help them to see that this is ok. In this chapter, we want to look to scripture for wisdom to help us in our decision making. Students may say they would find out details not given in the reading to help make a decision. These factors may include Amanda's job satisfaction in her current role and if she would enjoy this campus job.

Chapter 4 – Thanksgiving Break

Daniel, a resident advisor, is the focus of this chapter. He finds himself alone in the residence hall on Thanksgiving weekend due to a snowstorm. In the hectic lives we lead, it is rare to find ourselves in a place of quiet solitude. This can be especially true for students living on campus or in an apartment setting. Whether in a classroom or a residence hall room, we are almost always around people. People are at the store when we go grocery shopping. We are around others in the cafeteria when we eat our meals there. Even in our cars, the radio can fill an otherwise silent space.

In your discussion, help your group members to consider the spiritual discipline of solitude. Spending time in silence and solitude may produce a strange feeling at first since we are accustomed to being around people or having some sort of background noise such as music or television. We can be confident, however, that there is value in setting aside time to spend in solitude. We know this because we see Jesus model it in his actions. Solitude provides a time to pray, spend time in scripture, and reflect on what God is doing in our lives.

A psalm that specifically mentions meditating is in the scripture reading. Psalms can provide excellent passages to read during times of solitude. In them, we can find a variety of emotions expressed. Some were written out of gratitude to God, while others express confusion or even anger. The other scripture verses show how Jesus modeled taking time to be alone with God.

Daniel unexpectedly benefits from his time of solitude when he considers his real feelings about God. He sees other benefits when he takes time to consider what his next steps will be after graduating. You can model this for your group members by sharing what you do when you need time alone. If this is not a current discipline in your life, you can share with your group how you plan to incorporate times of silence and solitude into your schedule.

The challenge for this week involves spending time reading over the scripture verses. Mark your calendar for one month from the day you cover this lesson. Take some time to discuss any insights group members gained during this time.

Chapter 5 – Christmas Break

Here, we find Brandon catching up with his friends over Christmas break. It is exciting to not only hear everything new with his friends but also to share what is new in his life. There are several directions the conversation about this chapter may go.

Brandon is concerned about Jacob after hearing about his first semester. Use your time to discuss the benefits of surrounding yourself with a strong support situation and being careful to surround yourself with positive influences. You might also highlight the importance of not putting yourself in situations where you might be tempted to make bad choices.

The scripture from Matthew talks about how we are to confront other believers when there is a disagreement. Lead your group in a discussion of Brandon's responsibility to Jacob as well as to himself. It is important to encourage our friends and set an example of Christ's love in our behavior. But we must also know where we struggle with temptation and should avoid those situations. How can Brandon find the right balance?

Another topic of discussion is the presence of social media. Our social media accounts usually include posts and pictures highlighting the fun things we do. In reality, life is not always perfect. We all have struggles, but looking at social media can give the impression that everyone else is living a great life. Use your group's time to discuss why this can be harmful.

A third source of conversation concerns how we grow and change over time. As we meet new people and try new things, the decisions we make shape who we become. The familiarity of places like Jake's Diner gives Brandon a sense of gratitude, and he is thankful for the time to reconnect with his friends. With Jacob, however, we see how quickly we can change based on the decisions we make. You might take time to explore how some of the people we meet are in our lives for a season and some become our forever friends. Discuss why it is important to both be a dependable friend and to have friends who you can depend on during difficult times.

Chapter 6 – When You Don't Quite Fit In

Students have returned to begin the spring semester in this chapter. To welcome everyone back, the university is holding an overnight lock-in. One group from Campus Christian Assembly is meeting at the event while another group is going bowling first. One student, Ethan, is a nice guy but can get on people's nerves. He is the focus of this chapter, as well as how he is treated by the different student groups.

In your discussion, help students to look at this from the different points of view. The group meeting at the lock-in gave an open invitation to everyone but didn't specifically invite

Ethan. If you were this group, you may not feel like you need to speak to everyone individually. Consider what you would do if you were part of this group.

Brandon and Austin did extend an invitation to Ethan. As the two walked back to their residence hall, they joke about the fact that Ethan can be annoying. Do you see this as wrong or just acknowledging a truth about Ethan?

Finally, we must consider Ethan. What is his responsibility here? It might help to share with the group about a time when you were new to a group. When there are activities designed to fellowship and get to know each other, what is your responsibility as someone new to a group? As you discuss, remember that everyone's personality is different. People range from extremely outgoing to very shy. Then there are those people like Ethan who are socially awkward and struggle to fit in.

As we meet people, some become very close friends while others may only be acquaintances. We don't have to invite every person to every event. However, at planned events like the lock-in, it is important to help people to feel welcome. If you find that a group you belong to is not welcoming or friendly, ask yourself "Am I welcoming?" and "Am I friendly?".

Chapter 7 – Spring Break

A group of students in this chapter are spending their spring break on a service trip. This story provides a great opportunity to discuss the saying "It is better to give than to receive." The discussion questions will provide opportunities for students to share meaningful experiences they have had serving and volunteering. Some group members may struggle to think of ways they have served others. Help them to remember that meaningful service does not have to be a huge act. It can be as simple as checking on a friend going through a rough time, treating employees at stores and restaurants with respect, or volunteering your time to charitable organizations. Meaningful service can even be helping you as the group facilitator by participating in the discussion of each chapter!

Everyone except Lauren is focused on productivity. Help your group to see that their motives are not bad. By working hard, more items can be sorted and distributed to families that need those items. Lauren, however, is able to see an opportunity the others miss. As you read the scripture for this chapter, point out that Jesus was not in a hurry. That does not mean he was lazy. It also does not mean that we should just ignore the practical work that needs to be done.

Use part of your time to discuss how you would seek the right balance between being productive and taking time to build relationships. The staff at the warehouse is greatly encouraged when the students invest some time getting to know them. The students also seem to enjoy their time better.

Chapter 8 – Goodbye Winter, Hello Spring!

This chapter may be awkward to discuss. The focus is on lust and the respect we are to show members of the opposite sex. It may be to your benefit to acknowledge this awkwardness at the beginning of your time together. Group members may be relieved to know that everyone probably feels uneasy about discussing this lesson.

There will likely be a variety of viewpoints shared during discussion. Remind everyone to be respectful of differing views and pray for wisdom as we determine the best way to conduct ourselves as representatives of Christ.

Part of your conversation will explore the responsibilities men and women have. Each of us has a responsibility to behave responsibly. That means being respectful in what we say to members of the opposite sex. It also means monitoring how we look at people we find attractive. Physical attraction is a normal part of life and an important part of a relationship. Our eyes are going to be drawn to people we find attractive. However, we must be aware of how long we look and be wary of our thoughts when we see find ourselves physically attracted to someone. Factors like the person's character and whether they have a relationship with Christ matter greatly. We must ask if someone we wish to date would be a supportive partner.

They most volatile part of the study may come when the discussion turns to how we are to dress. Some students may say that we should dress modestly so we do not lead anyone to thoughts that do not honor God. Others may feel they can dress as they please, and it is each person's responsibility to monitor their own thoughts and actions. Encourage group members to consider how the way we dress can honor or dishonor God. Also consider how our choice of clothing may become a stumbling block for those around us.

You may consider spending part of this lesson separated by gender. The men and women in your group may feel more comfortable sharing if they are only with other members of the same gender. If time allows, split the group by gender to go through the discussion questions. Ask someone of the opposite sex to help guide the other group's discussion. Then come back as a large group and go through the questions again.

Chapter 9 – Leadership Team

This chapter focuses on Lauren as she chooses a way she would like to serve in the next school year. There is a great opportunity in this chapter to have your group perform a spiritual gifts inventory. There are many available either online or in paper format. Work with a campus minister or church leader to identify one to use with this lesson. Based on the time constraints of your group, you might have them do this before this week's lesson.

We are taught to be humble and not speak highly of ourselves. For this reason, some group members may feel uncomfortable sharing their strengths. Point out that our gifts come from God and it is okay to share our strengths with the group.

Others may not feel they are strong in any of the areas mentioned in the scripture reading. Hopefully, the inventory will help them see some areas where they have potential. Consider having group members write down strengths they see in other group members. This could be done aloud while your group is together. You could also ask your group to do this anonymously and write down gifts they see in each other. It might be surprising to discover in which areas others perceive you to be strong. Allow some time for your group to discuss the results. Are there areas of overlap among the inventory results, your own self-analysis, and what others perceive to be your gifts?

Group members may also learn about themselves as they rank the four choices that Lauren has. Based on their rankings, ask follow up questions about what their rankings can teach them about their interests. As your discussion progresses, make sure that everyone in the group is included. If group members take time to share the gifts they see in each other, ensuring everyone feels included will be especially important. No one should leave this week's study feeling they are unimportant. Help encourage everyone so they know that we each have at least one gift, and no one's gift is more important than anyone else's.

Chapter 10 – The Catalyst

Catalysts are the focus of this chapter. A catalyst can be defined as a person or thing that precipitates an event. Catalysts take initiative. They resist passivity, whether changing something with themselves internally or addressing an external situation. When they see a need, they do something. Catalysts ask "How can I make this better?".

We see catalysts throughout this chapter. When Michelle hears Amanda describing a desire to find ways to serve and grow, she tells Steve that Amanda might be a good fit for the summer staff position his friend is trying to fill. Steve and Michelle are catalysts for Amanda, telling her about the position and encouraging her by describing the gifts that would help her succeed in the role. If Amanda chooses to apply and is selected, she could be a catalyst for the groups she would work with over the summer. By simply getting to know them, encourage them, and share her faith with them, she could be a catalyst in their spiritual growth.

In the story, Michelle mentions a study she and Amanda were both part of that covered the book of Ezra. The scripture verses for this chapter are all from Ezra. Ezra is a biblical example of a catalyst. In order to give your group proper context, take time before reading the scripture verses to share the following overview of the timeline of events leading up to Ezra's arrival in Jerusalem.

The people of Israel and Judah had fallen away from God. The prophet Jeremiah had told them they would be overthrown and taken captive. The events Jeremiah prophesized came to pass and the people of Israel spent decades in captivity. Through God's mercy, the people of Israel were eventually allowed to rebuild their temple and return to their homeland. However, they fell back into their sinful ways. This is where Ezra finds them. Because Ezra takes action, the Israelites turn away from their sinful practices. Ezra is a catalyst. A group of Israelites seen in the tenth chapter serves as catalysts for Ezra by telling Ezra they will support him.

One of the discussion questions challenges group members to look at situations in their own lives where they might be able to serve as a catalyst. However, we must use wisdom and discernment to know if it is appropriate for us to get involved. Group members may struggle to know if and when they should do something.

There are many ways group members can answer this question. One way is to simply pray about a given situation. This is something we see Ezra do. We can also pray for the specific people involved. Asking God to help others is a way we can be a catalyst. Ask the members of your group to look at their motives for getting involved. Is their motive truly to try and make things better? Or do they want to get involved for less honorable reasons, such as creating conflict or being nosy? If the motive is truly to make things better, ask group members if the situation is in their sphere of influence? Are they in a position to get involved and help? If not, is there someone in a better position to address the situation that they could help and support? This is another way that we can be catalysts.

Understanding the events leading up to the book of Ezra will be important to fully appreciating this chapter. It will also be important to help your group understand why Ezra was able to help. The scripture verses tell us that Ezra had studied, practiced, and taught the Law. Reading and studying scripture help us gain wisdom and learn ways to model God's love. Practicing God's love is tough. It requires us to show kindness, patience, and mercy when we may not feel like it. It takes prayer and the help of the Holy Spirit to model God's love in our actions. Teaching about Jesus can be done in different ways. We can lead Bible studies. We can serve in various ministries. We can invest in relationships that hopefully leads to opportunities to share our faith. Ezra's prior studying, practicing, and teaching had prepared him to be a catalyst.

This chapter helps pull wisdom from a book of the Bible your group may not have spent much time studying. It shows how we can prepare now to be useful catalysts for God throughout our lives. Encourage your group members to know they have what it takes to serve God in mighty ways.

Chapter 11 – Dead Week Decisions

Brandon spends this chapter considering how he wants to spend his summer. The discussion questions provide an opportunity to work through each option and weigh the pros and cons of each. Some group members may feel pressure to choose serving as a camp counselor because they feel it is a "church answer." However, we can live our lives in a way that honors Christ wherever we are.

There is an opportunity here to tie in lessons from other chapters. In chapter five, Brandon was concerned about how Jacob had changed during the first semester of college. Working either full or part time in his hometown might give him a chance to reconnect with Jacob. In chapter seven, we learned that sometimes the mission is not the mission. As a camp counselor, you can build relationships with your campers. However, you will also have opportunities to build relationships with coworkers at either the full-time landscaping job or any part-time job you get. This is not to say that you say that working at the camp is a bad choice. Rather, it is to point out that no one should feel pressured to choose this option.

As in previous chapters, your group members may choose different options. Make sure everyone knows this is just a reflection of our different gifts and preferences. As long as you thoughtfully consider each option and seek to honor God in whatever you choose, it is perfectly fine that not everyone chooses the same option.

The challenge for this lesson is to memorize the scripture verses for the chapter. Discuss how many of the verses group members can commit to memorize by the time you meet for the next lesson. Encourage group members when you see them throughout the week.

Chapter 12 – Going Home, Leaving Home

The final chapter finds Austin reflecting on his first year of college. Use this time to help your group members reflect on their past, present, and future. Revisit your conversation from chapter one about the biggest concerns you had as an incoming freshman. How did those turn out? Consider your present situation. Has your definition of home and family changed? Then look to the future. What are your concerns about next semester and how you will spend the time between semesters? Guide your group members to remember that they made it through the beginning of school and can trust God to help in the future.

One question asks who group members will look to for support over the summer. Brandon had a support system in high school but was worried about having one in college. Some group members may have the opposite problem. They may have found a stronger support system now that they will have over the summer. Allow group members to share what individuals in this situation might do so no one leaves school feeling isolated and alone.

After going through the discussion questions, take time to discuss the major takeaways from this study as a whole. My hope is that group members realize that God made us to be decision makers. We will each make choices, and they may be different than someone else's decision in the same circumstance. But there is nothing wrong with that as long as we seek to honor God in the decisions we make. The Bible may not tell us where to live or which major to choose. It can, however, equip us with the wisdom to make those decisions for ourselves.

Thank you for facilitating the conversation in this study. The freshman year of college can be simultaneously exciting and scary. I hope this book has been beneficial to your group members and served as a catalyst for healthy conversations.

www.ingramcontent.com/pod-product-compliance
Lightning Source LLC
LaVergne TN
LVHW051836080426
835512LV00018B/2912